A LANCASHIRE TREASURY

Stories and folk-tales
of old Lancashire

WILLIAM E. A. AXON

© Aurora Publishing

ISBN 1 85926 057 8

published by
Aurora Enterprises Limited
Unit 9, Bradley Fold Trading Estate,
Radcliffe Moor Road, Bradley Fold,
Bolton BL2 6RT.
Tel: 01204 – 370 753/2
Fax: 01204 – 370 751

Edited by
Dawn Robinson-Walsh

Typeset, printed and bound by
Manchester Free Press,
Longford Trading Estate,
Thomas Street, Stretford,
Manchester M32 0JT.
Tel: 0161 – 864 4540
Fax: 0161 – 866 9866

PREFACE

Being too many for me to reckon up or remember, it will be the safest way to wrap them altogether in some Manchester ticking, and to fasten them with pins, (to prevent their falling out or scattering), or tie them with tape, and also because sure bind, sure find, to bind them about with points and laces, all made at the same place.

THOMAS FULLER, D.D.

EVEN when the historian has told in the most elaborate detail the story of the County Palatine of Lancaster, there still remains much that is noteworthy. There are pleasant byways of family history and biography to be explored, quaint fancies and dark superstitions to be recorded, and many notable incidents and curious events to be chronicled. In this volume an attempt has been made to indicate some of the characteristics of the past history and condition of the county. "Lancashire fair women," the old proverb speaks of, and these have never lacked their complement of brave men whose valour has sometimes been that of the warrior leading his soldiers to victory, sometimes that of the sectary scorning the persecutions of the world, sometimes of the inventor struggling against the neglect and greed of his fellows, and sometimes—alas! for the intolerance of human nature that it should be so—this native courage has been shown by the pale martyr in his sheet of fire.

The historical associations of the county connect it with some of the most momentous epochs in the life of the nation, and its halls, farmhouses, and cottages have given soldiers to the field, statesmen to the senate, and preachers to the churches. The manifestations of this quick, vigorous life furnish the subjects of several articles in this volume.

The folk-lore and dialect of the county are unusually rich, and the connection of some of its fireside stories and familiar customs with those of other lands have been shown.

Some of the articles now reprinted have been read before the Royal Society of Literature, the Historic Society of Lancashire and Cheshire, and the Manchester Literary Club; some have appeared in the *Academy,* the *Manchester Guardian, Notes and Queries,* the *Palatine Notebook,* and various periodicals, whilst others are now printed for the first time. The volume is a selection from much more extensive materials relating to the history and archæology of Lancashire, and which may possibly be further drawn upon in the future.

CONTENTS

LANCASHIRE GLEANINGS.

NANNY CUTLER, A LANCASHIRE "DINAH BEDE."

This seemed a strange idea for Methodists, some of whose brightest ornaments have been women preachers. As far back as Adam Clarke's time, his objections were met by the answer, 'If an *ass* reproved Balaam, and a *barn-door fowl* reproved Peter, why shouldn't a *woman* reprove sin?' This classification with donkeys and fowls is certainly not very complimentary. The first comparison I heard wittily replied to by a coloured woman who had once been a slave. 'May-be a speaking woman *is* like an ass,' said she; 'but I can tell you one thing —the ass saw the angel, when Balaam didn't.'—MRS. CHILD, *Letters from New York.*

IN Methodist circles the name of Nanny Cutler is still heard, but it may be doubted if the general public have any particular knowledge of a woman who was remarkable among that class of which the Dinah Morris of George Eliot is a type.

Ann Cutler was born near Preston in 1759, and the record of her life shows her to have been one of those "fair souls" of whom Carlyle speaks. She grew up a quiet and serious girl, but it was not until she was 26, that during the visit of some Methodist preachers, in the phraseology of the sect, she "was convinced of sin," and, after a brief interval, "found a sinking in humility, love, and dependence upon God." She is described as having "a smile of sweet composure, which seemed, in a sense, a reflection of the Divine Nature." The ministry of women was not acknowledged amongst the Methodists of that day, and her evident vocation for prayer and preaching was a source of trouble, and brought her some reproach. "I cannot," she said, "be happy unless I cry for sinners. I do not want any praise: I want nothing but souls to be brought to God. I am reproached by most. I cannot do it to be seen or heard of men. I see the world going to destruction, and I am burdened till I pour out my soul to God for them." The charm of her praying seemed to be in the intense force of her sympathy for the sinful, and for those who were immersed in the cares and pleasures of the daily life. It was for these that she cried aloud and spared not. Mr. Taft tells us that many were astonished that such great results should be produced by one so weak and in appearance so insignificant.

The simplicity of her own daily existence was not without a tinge of asceticism. Her diet consisted chiefly of milk and such herb-tea as in those days was common amongst the country folk. On this simple fare she was able to go through great exertions. She arose at midnight for an interval of prayer, and her usual time of rising for the day was at four o'clock, as the light began to dawn. The ascetic spirit was probably also the motive of the resolution which devoted her to a celibate life. Amongst the many papers she left behind was one in which she thus "vowed" herself. In an age when "Methodist" was a term of reproach, and when the vilest slanders were freely circulated, the fair fame of Ann Cutler remained unassailed. She was not gloomy, though but little given to conversation, and some of her "experiences" were of so remarkable a nature, that she forbore, and wisely, to speak of them in public. The manner of mystics all over the world is the same, and it would be an unwise curiosity that would pry closely into the exact nature of what Ann Cutler believed was her continual fellowship and union with the Deity. She mentioned the matter to John Wesley, and his reply is interesting and judicious.

"WALTON, APRIL 15, 1790.

"My Dear Sister,

"There is something in the dealings of God with your soul which is out of the common way. But I have known several whom He has been pleased to lead in exactly the same way, and particularly in manifesting to them distinctly the three Persons of the ever blessed Deity. You may tell all your experience to me at any time; but you will need to be cautious in speaking to others, for they would not understand what you say. Go on in the name of God, and in the power of His might. Pray for the whole spirit of humility, and I wish that you would write and speak without reserve to, dear Nanny,

"Yours affectionately,

"JOHN WESLEY."

This letter is not included in the collected correspondence of the founder of Methodism, and his diary is defective at this very point, a portion of the record for April, 1790, having been lost.   The sect were unwilling to admit women as preachers and teachers, and Ann Cutler had therefore much to endure.   Her biographer, the Rev. William Bramwell, says: " She met with the greatest opposition that I ever knew one person to receive, and I never saw or heard of her being in the least angry.   She never complained of ill usage. She was sent for by many, both rich and poor; and though she was exceedingly sensible of opposition, yet she would say : I am not received at such a place ; but the will of the Lord be done."   Mr. Bramwell at times thought proper to dissuade her from undertaking the work of a revivalist, but on some occasions she felt it her duty to go and speak to the people from the full sympathy of her pure and womanly heart.   The flock for whom he was labouring had their full share of the benefit of her singular power.   It is, of course, known now that Dinah Morris was in a large measure a portrait of Elizabeth Evans, the aunt of the novelist.   It was while listening to a prayer by Mr. Bramwell, that Elizabeth Evans " found peace."   Under the influence of Nanny Cutler there was a great "revival" at Dewsbury, and it spread to Birstall, Leeds, Bradford, and Otley.   Nor was her native county neglected.   Her last journey was to Oldham, Manchester, Derby, and Macclesfield.   From Manchester she wrote an enthusiastic letter to her sister. " The last week but this," she says, "at Oldham, and Delph, and another place, near a hundred souls were brought to

God. Many cried for mercy and the Lord delivered them. In this town I cannot exactly tell the number. God has sanctified many; some preachers and leaders." This was at the end of November and the beginning of December, 1794, and in the following month she went to Macclesfield, and there, in spite of gathering illness, she continued to preach and pray, to visit the sick and to labour in the task to which she had devoted her strong soul. She had a presentiment that the end was not far off. "I long to see Abraham, Isaac, Jacob, Wesley, Fletcher, and some other dear friends that I have known on earth." Her illness increased, and on the 29th she died, about six o'clock in the winter afternoon.

Dr. Aspden, of Blackburn, was with her at the last. "Nanny, how are you?" he asked. "I am very ill," she replied faintly. "You are, but I trust your soul is perfectly happy." "Yes, it is," she rejoined, "but I cannot so fully rejoice because of the weight of my affliction." "Well, the Lord does not require it, or He would give strength." "Yes," she replied, "He would, glory be to God and the Lamb for ever." These were her last words.

Ann Cutler was buried in the graveyard of Christ's Church, Macclesfield, of which that extraordinary man the Rev. David Simpson was then minister. A copper plate was fixed upon her tombstone, with the following inscription :—

Underneath lie the remains of

ANN CUTLER,

Whose simple manner, solid piety, and
extraordinary power in prayer, distinguished and

rendered her eminently useful in promoting a religious
revival wherever she came.

She was born near Preston, in Lancashire, and
died here December 29th, 1794.

Æ. 35.

It was probably the memory of Nanny Cutler that led
Mr. Bramwell to ask in a sermon that was heard by Elizabeth
Evans, "Why are there not more women preachers?"
" Because they are not faithful to their call."

There are two editions of the biography of this saintly
woman. " A short account of the life and death of Ann
Cutler," by Mr. William Bramwell, was printed at Sheffield
in 1796, and reprinted at York in 1827, with a preface by
Mr. Z. Taft, and some additional matter. The mystical
element in Methodism was evidenced not only by such lives as
that of Nanny Cutler, but by the trance or visions of Elizabeth
Dickinson, in the year 1792. This delicate Yorkshire girl
who died the year before Ann Cutler, and in her twentieth
year, sometimes had the strength given by enthusiasm, that
enabled her to address audiences of more than a thousand
people. One of her converts was a consumptive girl named
Proctor, who died in 1794. As she lay upon her death-bed
one of the class leaders who had been watching with her,
through the night, was returning home through the darkness
of a winter morning. It was about four o'clock, and he was
walking over the fields. " Suddenly " (the rest we must give
in Mr. Bramwell's words), " a light shone around him, which
eclipsed and put out the light derived from his lantern ; he
looked up and saw four angels, in company with Betty

Dickinson, whose face he saw as clearly, and knew as perfectly, as he did while she was living, and she had a golden girdle about her loins. They were flying swiftly in the direction of Miss Proctor's house. The next morning he heard that Miss Proctor had died soon after he left her." A sceptical age must be left to place what interpretation it pleases upon the vision of an enthusiast, overwrought by long vigil at the sick bed of a dying girl.

Ann Cutler and Elizabeth Dickinson were not by any means the only Methodist women preachers. "Sister" Ryan, "Sister" Crosby, "Sister" Hurrell, "Sister" Bosanquitt, (who afterwards became Mrs. Fletcher), Mary Barritt, and others used their talents. John Wesley had a prejudice against the preaching of women, but he acknowledged that in special cases it would be wrong to prohibit them. "I think," he wrote to Sister Bosanquitt, "the strength of the cause rests here, in having an extraordinary call; so I am persuaded has every one of our lay-preachers; otherwise I could not countenance his preaching at all." This was in 1771. Mary Barritt preached in Manchester at the close of the last century, and one of her converts has left a somewhat vivid account of the effect of her open-air sermons at Shude Hill.

None of these preachers of the gentler sex were more remarkable than a little Lancashire girl of whom Charles Hulbert in "Museum Europæum" (p. 435) gives the following account :—

"Elizabeth Bradbury, who was born of poor parents at Oldham, Lancashire (as far as he recollects, in the year 1798). At the age of nine months she could almost articu-

late every word in common occurrence; with the sole
instruction of her mother.   At twelve months she could
read, and shortly after learned to write, and acquired some
knowledge of the Latin language.   At the age of three years
she stood upon a table placed in the pulpit of the Methodist
Chapel, Middleton, seven miles from Manchester, and
preached to a numerous and respectable congregation; the
effect upon the minds of the hearers was most extraordinary,
some absolutely fainted from excess of feeling and surprise.
She was at this period considered as a prodigy, or rather as
one endowed with miraculous gifts.   The crowds who came
daily to visit her, and the money which was presented to her
parents from visitors, prevented their acceptance of numerous offers from respectable individuals to take this extraordinary child under their protection, and to provide for her
education and future happiness.   About the year 1803 the
editor saw her at the 'Bull's Head,' Swinton, five miles from
Manchester, where her imprudent father exhibited her as a
prodigy of talent and literature, and induced her to act the
preacher for the amusement of public-house company.   She
appeared equally playful as other children of her years, but
seemed remarkably shrewd in her observations on the different characters in the company, especially on those who
were not quite so liberal in their gratuities as she could wish.
The editor requested her to write something in his pocket-
book as a proof of her talents, when she immediately wrote
her own and her father's name with each hand (right and
left) in a most beautiful style.   He has had no information
respecting her since the above period."

THE EXTRAORDINARY MEMORY OF THE

REV. THOMAS THRELKELD.

Memory, the warder of the brain.—SHAKSPERE.

AMONGST the worthies of Lancashire we may reckon
the Rev. Thomas Threlkeld, for 28 years the minister
of a Dissenting congregation in Rochdale, and remarkable
for his very unusual powers of memory. He was born
April 12, 1739, at Halifax, where his father was minister of
a Presbyterian church. Of his early education we have no
record, but "after his grammar learning was finished he
went first to the academy at Daventry," of which Doddridge
was once principal, and afterwards to the academy at
Warrington. This institution commenced in 1757, and
Threlkeld was a student there soon after the opening.

In 1762 he became a minister at Risley, near Warrington,
"with a small and plain, but most harmonious, affectionate,
and agreeable society of Presbyterian Dissenters." Here
he married Miss Martha Wright, the daughter of one of

his congregation.   In 1778 he removed to Rochdale, where, after 28 years of ministerial work, he died April 6, 1806.

After this brief sketch of Threlkeld's uneventful life we turn to consider his extraordinary acquirements.   When he first went to the Daventry academy, he could, on any passage of the Bible being recited, at once, and without hesitation, name the chapter and verse where it was to be found ; and if chapter and verse were named he was able at once to repeat the words.   His powers in this respect were often tested by his fellow-students, and were never known to fail. One of his contemporaries at Warrington was the Rev. Thomas Barnes, D.D., then of course only a student.   Mr. Barnes, with no thought of testing Mr. Threlkeld's powers, told an anecdote of " a parish clerk, who, having occasion to read the words ' Gebal, and Ammon, and Amalek,' sung them out in a manner so ridiculous that no person could have heard him without a smile.   Mr. T. immediately replied, ' These verses are in the 83rd Psalm and 7th verse.' And then joined most heartily in the laugh which he had himself unconsciously heightened by the oddness and gravity of his quotation."   Dr. Enfield once challenged him to tell the place of a text upon which he had been preaching. Mr. T. asked for a Bible and found the passage, saying, " Quote fair, sir, and you shall have a fair answer.   But I knew that you had confounded two verses together, which stand at a considerable distance asunder.   You have joined the 5th and 10th verses as though they were one.   I knew your trick, and I asked for the Bible that the company might with their own eyes detect you."

So firmly was Threlkeld's reputation established as a living concordance that in the latter years of his life his clerical brethren ceased to "amuse themselves by these experiments," in which he was uniformly successful. His powers of memory were often tested in other directions, and were never known to play false. As one of the managers of the fund for the benefit of the widows of Presbyterian ministers he was often appealed to on matters connected with the lives of deceased ministers, "and such was the opinion of his accuracy that if the books had been consulted, and had reported differently, the error would have been imputed to the secretary, and not to Mr. T's memory. This was deemed infallible."

Mr. Threlkeld was also a linguist. "Nine or ten languages it is certainly known that he read, not merely without difficulty, but with profound and critical skill." There is often a tendency to over-rate the number of languages acquired by individuals, but this statement appears to be made with due deliberation, and a critical knowledge of nine distinct tongues entitles the individual possessing it to rank only one degree lower than Mezzofanti and Sir William Jones. Mr. Threlkeld had books in the following languages, with all of which he is supposed to have had some acquaintance :—"English, Latin, Greek, Hebrew, with its dialects ; French, Italian, Spanish, German, Welsh, Dutch, Swedish, Gaelic, Manx, Arabic, Portuguese, Danish, Flemish." With the Greek Testament he was as familiar as with its English translation, and could quote and refer to chapter and verse with the same facility. His knowledge of Hebrew was profound.

There is an anecdote illustrative of his extreme fondness

for the Welsh language, with which he was well acquainted. When Dr. Priestley went to Wrexham to marry Miss Wilkinson he was accompanied by Mr. Threlkeld, who was to act as parent and give the bride away. The marriage service commenced and all went on well until the clergyman inquired who giveth this woman to be married to this man? when, to the consternation of the marriage party, the deputy-father was nowhere to be seen. A search at once began, and they found him at last buried in a large and lofty pew, where the charms of a Welsh Bible had caused him to forget everything else! His powers of recollection were not confined to words. Historical dates he remembered with equal accuracy, and was familiar with the details of chronology, heraldry, and genealogy, which were favourite amusements of his; and he could go through the pedigrees of many distinguished families, trace the succession of all the Episcopal Sees, and in other ways show his remarkable familiarity with family history. "But the most distinguishing excellence of Mr. T.'s memory lay in biography." He had long collected all the dates he could, not only concerning persons mentioned in history, but of every one of whom he could learn any facts. He had a passion for acquiring dates of events. To know when a person was born or married was a source of gratification to him apart from the importance or otherwise of the person. He revelled in these "smallbeer chronicles," and was always happy in the acquisition of this minute knowledge. His taste for inquiries of this sort must sometimes have been mistaken for a desire to pry into family affairs by those unable to

conceive of the pleasure to be derived from a simple knowledge of facts. Mr. Threlkeld in other respects appears to
have been a man of fair average abilities. He was extremely
modest, and had the simplicity of a child when apart from
his books. In fact, from the description we have of him,
he would appear to have been a good-hearted, awkward
scholar, as gentle and as ungainly as Dominie Sampson.
He was so short-sighted that he did not dare to ride on
horseback, because in that elevated position he could not
see the ground. The extreme shortness of his sight, no
doubt, added to his shyness and helplessness.

Dr. Barnes, from whom all these details have been drawn,
often tried to discover the *method* by which his friend was enabled to command the immense army of facts with which his
mind was stored. " Mr. T. told him that he classed them
together by the year, and referred every new entry to that
which lay nearest to it. He endeavoured to explain himself
by saying, ' The year you have just mentioned was 1631.
In that year Mr. Philip Henry was born. I have, therefore,
laid up that name along with his ; and they are now so
associated that whilst I retain the one I shall not forget the
other.'" This explanation does not throw much light upon
the matter, beyond the fact that it shows his method to
have depended upon the association of ideas. " From his
description," says Dr. Barnes, " so far as I could understand
it, his mind appeared to be divided and fitted up like a
shop, furnished with shelves and drawers for every different
kind of articles, so that every new article was immediately
referred to its own place, and so joined with those which

stood there before, that the whole row presented itself at
once, like soldiers drawn up in a line." This is certainly
one of the most remarkable cases of extraordinary memory
on record, and it rests upon very good evidence.

Dr. Barnes drew up a notice of Mr. Threlkeld, which was
read before the Literary and Philosophical Society of Manchester twenty years before that gentleman's death.   Dr.
Percival, Mr. Thomas Henry, and others who were members
of the Society, were also intimate with the subject of the
paper, and could confirm its statement from personal knowledge.   The diffidence and humility of Mr. Threlkeld were
the reasons why the paper was not printed in the memoirs
of the Society.   With all his prodigious knowledge, Threlkeld
never made any contribution to literature ; his great power
served no higher purpose than to excite the astonishment
and admiration of a small circle of friends.

The statements contained in this notice are made on the
authority of the following tract :—" A sermon preached at
Rochdale, April 13, 1806, on occasion of the death of the
Rev. Thomas Threlkeld, minister of a dissenting congregation in that place.   To which is added an appendix containing some account of the life and character of Mr.
Threlkeld, and particularly of the powers of memory, and
of the treasures of knowledge possessed by him.   By
Thomas Barnes, D.D., fellow of the American Philosophical
Society.   Manchester, printed by S. Russell, Deansgate.
1806."   Threlkeld is also alluded to, though not named, in
the preface to Priestley's " Index to the Bible," 1805.

ANN LEE,

THE MANCHESTER PROPHETESS.

And lean-look'd prophets whisper fearful change.—*Shakspere.*

THE Shakers, whose communistic villages are amongst the curiosities of America, owe their origin to a Manchester woman. Prophets are proverbially unhonoured in their own country. The smoky air of Manchester stifled the religious genius of Ann Lee; the boundless freedom of the New World was needed for its luxuriant growth. On the 29th of February, 1736, the family of John Lee, a blacksmith, living in Toad Lane (a name since euphemised into Todd Street), was increased by the advent of a little stranger, to whom the name of Ann was given. Mr. John Owen has kindly given me the following extracts from the Register of Baptisms at the Cathedral :—1734, April 16, Nancy, d. of John Lees; 1735, Jan. 11, Peter, son of John Lee; 1737, June 12, Betty, d. of John Lee; 1737, Aug. 21, Joseph, s. to John Lees; 1738, April 16, Thomas, s. to John Lees; 1741, May 10, Katherine, d. of John Leigh; 1741, June, Joseph, s. of John Lees, blacksmith; 1742, April 4, William,

s. of John Lees ; 1742, June 1, ANNE, d. of John Lee, was
privately baptised ; 1742, Feb. 13, Mary, d. of John Lees,
taylor ; 1743, Sept. 29, Sara, d. of John and Sarah Lee ;
1743, Oct. 9, WILLIAM, s. of John Lees, blacksmith ; 1746,
May, 4, Alice, d. of John Lees ; 1749, March 26, George, s.
of John Lees, blacksmith.   Like the family records of more
aristocratic houses, it is difficult to sort out the different
branches of the Lees, but the prophetess and her brother
are clearly distinguishable.

From the fact that she was privately "christened" when
six years old, we may perhaps infer that some serious illness
threatened her young life.   According to Shaker biography,
Ann's parents were hardworking, God fearing folk, who
brought up five sons and three daughters in the best way
they could as far as their light allowed them. Another statement would make it appear that the family were better
connected than might have been supposed from their poor
estate.   One of her uncles is said by Brown to have been a
sheriff of London and an alderman of "Aldgate Ward." The
same writer states, inaccurately, that General Charles Lee
was also her father's brother.

The schoolmaster was not abroad, and children were
packed off into the fields or the workroom instead of being
sent to master the mysteries of the "three R's."   So Ann,
we are told, was first employed in a cotton factory, then became a cutter of hatter's fur, and afterwards a cook in the
Manchester Infirmary, "where she was distinguished for her
neatness, faithfulness, and good economy." Her ways were
not those of other children, she lacked their keen joyfulness,

she was "serious and thoughtful," inclined to religious medi-
tations, and "often favoured with heavenly 'visions.'" In
1758 she became a member of a sect called Shakers, who
were "under the ministration of Jane and James Wardley,
formerly of the Quaker order," but who had left that body
about 1747.

The Manchester Shakers appear to have been a remnant
of the "French Prophets," who came into England about
1706. Charles Owen, in a work printed in 1712, alludes to
the secret meetings of some "prophets" in Manchester, and
to some providential check which they received. In their
fits of religious enthusiasm, when the Spirit entered into
them, they were seized with violent tremblings, and their
contortions gained them the nickname of Shakers. Wardley
was a tailor, who removed from Bolton to Cannon Street,
Manchester, where he lived with John Townley, a well-to-do
bricklayer. Jane Wardley, in the Shaker belief, was "evidently
the spirit of John the Baptist, or Elias, operating in the female
line, to prepare the way for the second appearing of Christ,
in the order of the female." The testimony of this woman
and her followers, according to what they saw by vision and
revelation from God was—"that the second appearing of
Christ was at hand, and that the Church was rising in her
full and transcendant glory, which would effect the final
downfall of antichrist." Another of the Shakers was John
Kattis, who was considered by them to be a good scholar.
He did not long retain his faith. (*Brown*, p. 312.)

Four years after joining this society, which numbered
about thirty people, Ann Lee was married. The entry in

the Cathedral registry is " 1762, Jan. 5, Abraham Standerin, blacksmith, and Ann Lees, married." James Shepherd and Thomas Hulme, signed as witnesses, but both bride and bridegroom affixed their marks, being unable to write. There is a pencil note in a copy of one of Robert Owen's publications in the Manchester Free Library, which states that she lived in Church Street, where Philip's warehouse now stands. The press mark of this tract is 17316 (63E. 12·7). The Shaker books, however, state, that after the marriage the young couple lived in the house of the bride's father in Toad Lane, during the time they remained in England. The Shaker biography gives the husband's name as Stanley, and states that four children were born unto them, who all died in infancy. To one of these the following entry from the Cathedral Burial Registry no doubt refers: " 1766, Oct. 7, Elizabeth, daughter of Abraham Standley." At the birth of her last child, forceps had to be used, and after the delivery, she lay for several hours apparently dead. (*Brown*, p. 312.) Her husband, it is said, was a drunkard, and treated her unkindly.

In 1766 the Shaker society was joined by John Hocknell, brother of Mrs. Townley, in whose house Jane Wardley lived. Hocknell was a substantial farmer near Maretown in Cheshire, and being zealous for the new faith, he gathered some of the poorer members into his own house, and there supported them. His wife, Hannah, not relishing this large accession of prophets, complained to her kindred (the Dickins family), and her three brothers sought the assistance of a magistrate, and "had John put in prison at Middlewich,

four miles from his own house." He escaped from tribula-
tion without any danger, and was rewarded by the conversion
of his wife, who "became a member of society and continued
through all the increase of the work, till she departed this
life, in America, sound in the faith of the Gospel, A.D.
1797." (*Testimony*, p. 616.) They used frequently to
meet "at John Partington's in Mayor-town [Maretown], as
they passed and repassed from Manchester to John
Hocknell's."

The small band of believers were looking for the Second
Advent, and there seems to have been an impression amongst
them that the Messiah would appear in the form of a woman.
It had been said of old that the Lord would shake not the
earth only, but also heaven. "The effects of Christ's first
appearing," says the Shaker *Testimony*, "were far from
fulfilling those promises in their full extent, for in reality
that heaven which was to be shaken, had not yet been
built, neither did the appearing of Christ in the form of a
man fulfil the desire of all nations. But a second appearing was to be manifested in woman, which completed the
desire of all nations, by the revelation of the Mother
Spirit in Christ, an emanation from the eternal Mother."
Creed these people do not appear to have had, simply a
strong conviction that the great day of the Lord was at hand,
and that he would reveal himself in the flesh and lead his
people to that peace which he had promised them of old.

Amongst this band of simple enthusiasts, the ignorant
blacksmith's daughter began to exert a powerful influence.
She is described as being of medium height and well-pro-

portioned.   Her fair complexion was lit up by blue eyes,
and set off by brown chestnut hair, whilst her mild countenance wore an aspect habitually grave.   Altogether a
solemn-looking, lowly-born, "fair saint."   Wifely and
motherly cares did not fill up the measure of her life, and
the loss of her children may have intensified the morbid
enthusiasm to which at all ages she would seem to have been
subjected.   She was a "seeker after salvation," and, passing
through a period of mental struggles, doubts, and perplexities,
she " was born into the spiritual kingdom."   This new stage
of her intellectual history was marked by the evolution of
the doctrine that complete celibacy was the true order of
the world and essential to individual salvation.   She considered it her duty to cry down the " fleshly lusts which war
against the soul," and, according to the Shaker book, was
imprisoned in consequence.   Although the increase of the
population was considered a matter of importance, it is
scarcely likely that the constables of Manchester would put
the mother of four children into jail for preaching celibacy,
and accordingly we find it stated further on that the charge
against them was that of Sabbath-breaking.   There can be
no doubt that the dancing, shouting, shaking, "speaking
with new tongues," and all the other wild evidences of religious fervour exhibited by Ann and her fellow-believers,
would be exceedingly distasteful to her neighbours and lead
to occasional displays of brutal intolerance.

It may not unnaturally be asked why, if Ann Lee was the
woman chosen to proclaim the gospel of celibacy, she should
herself have entered into the bonds of matrimony.   She

became a Shaker in 1758, and a wife in 1762. Clearly she was then unconscious of her great mission. This is confessed, for we are told that, although "from her childhood she had great light and conviction of the sinfulness and depravity of human nature," yet, "not having attained that knowledge of God, which she early desired . . . . she, being prevailed upon by the earnest solicitations of her relations and acquaintances, yielded reluctantly, was married, and had four children, all of whom died in infancy." The cause of her marriage, it will be seen, was that which has deluged the world with mediocre poetry—the solicitation of her friends.

The date of her first imprisonment is said to have been the year 1770, and, whilst "in bonds," her soul was gladdened by seeing "Jesus Christ in open vision, who revealed to her the most astonishing views of Divine manifestations of truth, in which she had a perfect and clear view of the mystery and iniquity, the root and foundation of all human depravity, and of the very act of transgression committed by Adam and Eve in the garden of Eden." Brown says, that in 1771 she became head of the Society, who joined with her in a "testimony against the lust of the flesh;" she was taken from a meeting and placed in a dungeon, next day sent to Bedlam, but after some weeks discharged.— (p. 312.) From this time her followers gave her the name of "Mother Ann," and looked upon her as the female complement of the risen Christ; or, to quote the exact words of Shakers—"from the light and power of God, which attended her ministry, and the certain power of salvation transmitted to those who received her testimony, she was received and acknowledged as the first Mother, or spiritual Parent in the line of the female, and the second Heir in the covenant of life, according to the present display of the gospel." (*Testimony*, p. 620.)

If the Shakers endured much cruelty from zealous Sabbatarians, it must be admitted that they were not eager to avoid giving offence.   Thus the *Manchester Mercury* of July 20th, 1773, tells us :—" Saturday last ended the Quarter Sessions, when John Townley, John Jackson, Betty Lees, and Ann Lees (Shakers), for going into Christ Church, in Manchester, and there wilfully and contemptuously, in the time of Divine service, disturbing the congregation then assembled at morning prayers in the said church, were severally fined £20 each."   Very probably the non-payment of this fine would be the cause of one of Mother Ann's imprisonments.   On one occasion, according to Elder Evans and other Shaker writers, " she was dragged out of the meeting by a mob, and cast into a prison in Manchester. They put her in a cell so small that she could not straighten herself, and with the design of starving her to death, kept her there fourteen days without food; nor was the door opened during all that time.   She had nothing to eat or drink, except some wine and milk mixed, put into the bowl of a tobacco-pipe, and conveyed to her, by inserting the stem through the keyhole, once every twenty-four hours. This was done by James Whittaker, when a boy, whom Mother Ann brought up."   This is a marvellous narrative, and our Shaker friends must excuse our incredulity.   It was never either law or custom to starve people to death for Sabbath-breaking. The nearest parallel we can find is that of the Puritan, who—

> Hanged his cat on the Monday,
> For killing a mouse upon Sunday.

Again, a cell with a keyhole looking into the street, is not a likely arrangement. In point of fact, in the House of Correction, which served as a jail, before the erection of New Bailey, the prisoners were not on the ground-floor at all, but a story higher, and it was a common thing for their friends to pass food through the window gratings to the caged birds inside. This arrangement is shown in the engraving which appears in Proctor's "Memorials of Manchester Streets," p. 13. It is copied from a drawing by Thomas Barritt, and represents the House of Correction as it was about 1776. The older prison on the bridge was doubtless a much worse place, but it will not agree any better with the story. The approximate date of Mother Ann's first imprisonment is given as 1770. This semi-miracle is as an example of the law of development. It is not always one has a chance of assisting at the birth of a myth.

At another time she was rescued from the raging multitude by a "nobleman," who, living at some distance, "was remarkably wrought upon in his mind" to go to a certain place, which he did, riding "as if it had been to save his own life." According to Elder Evans, the mob once took her before four clergymen and charged her with blasphemy, but she spoke before them "for four hours of the wonderful works of God," and "they testified that she had spoken in seventy-two different tongues." Without wishing to disparage the linguistic powers of the English clergy of a hundred years ago, it may be remarked that an average of eighteen languages, exclusive of duplicates, is rather too liberal an allowance for four people. The mob, we are further told, took Ann and three of her followers into a valley outside the town, with the intention of stoning them to death; they threw the stones, but did not succeed in hitting the fair saint," and fell to quarrelling amongst themselves, so she escaped. According to Dr. Dwight she claimed the title of Ann *the Word.* He adds, that she was confined in a madhouse. The Shaker biography represents her as having been a cook at the Manchester Infirmary, and as this was at that time also a Lunatic Hospital, both statements may be correct. "For two years previous to their leaving England, persecution entirely ceased," says Elder Evans. We have seen that they were in trouble in July, 1773, and "on the 19th of May, 1774, Mother Ann, Abraham Stanley (her husband), William. Lee, James Whittaker, John Hocknell, Richard Hocknell, James Shepherd (perhaps the witness of the marriage), Mary Partington, and Nancy Lee, embarked for America." The captain was annoyed at their queer religious exercises, and threatened to throw some of them overboard, but a storm springing up, the Shakers assured the seamen that they would not be wrecked although the ship had sprung a leak. They landed at New York, August 6th, 1774. The departure of the young prophetess led to the collapse of the Shakers in Manchester. James and

Jane Wardley left the house of their benefactor Townley, and soon found a resting place in the almshouse, where they died; and the other members of the society "who remained in England, being without lead, or protection, generally lost their power, and fell into the common course and practice of the world." (*Testimony*, p. 621.)

The object of this Shaker emigration is by no means clear. They did not at once form themselves into a colony, but divided in search of employment. Abraham Stanley not being a convert to the celibate creed, soon "married" another woman. It is grievous to learn that Abraham never was accounted entirely orthodox. His was a very difficult part to play. The husband of a celibate prophetess would need more discretion than one could expect from a black-smith who could not write his own name. He must have had some faith in her, or would scarcely have crossed the water along with her other disciples. He appears to have maintained an outward conformity to the new faith, and the final cause of his backsliding was a severe sickness, which he suffered in 1775. Through this illness, we are told, Mother Ann nursed him with every possible care. Whilst convalescent, and before strong enough to return to work, he began to frequent public houses, and there made ship-wreck of his faith, in the manner already indicated.

Shortly after Mother Ann removed to Albany, and thence to the place then called Neuskenna, but now known as Watervliet. This spot they are said to have selected by the advice of some Quakers in New York, to whom they applied for counsel. (*Brown*, p. 315.) Here the scattered believers united, and a "religious revival" having commenced at Lebanon, N.Y., in 1780, the Shakers increased in number, but were greatly persecuted on account of their testimony against war and oath-taking. A number of them, including Mother Ann, were arrested at Albany. They would not take the oath, because "the Spirit of Christ, which they had within them, both disposed and enabled them to keep every just law, without any external obligation." (*Testimony*, p. 625.) Their imprisonment was not of a very harsh nature, for their disciples were allowed access to them, and also permitted to minister "freely to their necessities." Through the prison gratings the captive prophets sometimes preached to listening crowds. The problem of disposing of their prisoners seems to have puzzled those who had placed them in jail. Mother Ann and Mary Partington were separated from the rest, and conveyed to the prison at Poughkeepsie. It is said, by Shaker writers, that the intention was to place her on board a vessel which was loading with supplies for the British army, then at New York. This is to say at least very improbable. (*Testimony*, p. 626.)

At last the treatment of these strange people was reported to the governor, George Clinton, and as there seemed to be no probability that the strong argument of a prison house would overcome their repugnance to bearing arms and taking oaths, he ordered the release of all those who were in bonds at Albany. Upon their release, about the 20th of December, they represented to him the case of Mother Ann, whose freedom took place about the end of the year. Their general opposition was mistaken for a special aversion to the war of the revolution, and their refusal to take oaths was construed into a feeling in favour of the British arms; so that the alleged motive for their imprisonment at Albany was that of high treason in communicating with the British lines. There was no evidence in support of this charge, and hence her release by Governor Clinton. (Drake's *American Biog.*, Art. LEE.) Twenty years after this event the Governor visited the settlement at New Lebanon, and expressed to the believers there his satisfaction at having released their spiritual Mother from durance vile. (*Testimony*, p. 626.)

In 1781, Mother Ann and the elders went forth upon a missionary tour, visiting the believers wherever they were known, and preaching their peculiar doctrines wherever an opportunity occurred. They gained a number of converts at Harvard, Massachusetts, amongst the "Shadrach Irelands," so named from Shadrach Ireland, their leader. These people had renounced their wives; but as soon as they became perfectly free from sin, they might "marry spiritual wives, from whom were to proceed holy children, which were to constitute the New Jerusalem or Millennium." The chief of the sect had put away his own and taken a spiritual wife. He said he should not die; or if he did, he should rise again on the third day. He did die, but he did not rise again on the third day. "In these journeys," say the Shaker *Testimony*, "they were much persecuted and abused by the wicked oppressors of the truth," being sometimes whipped out of the towns.

What the world thought of this mission will be seen from the statements made to Dr. Dwight :—" In this excursion, she is said to have collected from her followers all their plate, ear-rings, and other ornaments which were formed of silver, gold, or gems." Dr. Dwight further says : "This woman has laboured under very serious imputations. In a book, published by Mr. Rathbone, he mentions that he found her, and one of these elders in very suspicious circumstances. She professed that she was inspired ; that she carried on a continual intercourse with the invisible world, and talked familiarly with angels. She predicted in the boldest terms, that the world would be destroyed at a given time : if I remember right, the year 1783. During the interval between the prophecy and its expected fulfilment, she directed them to cease from their common occupations. The direction was implicitly obeyed. As the earth, however, presented no appearance of dissolution, and the sky no signs of a conflagration, it was discovered that the prophecy had been miscalculated ; and her followers were ordered again to their employments. From that period they have been eminently industrious."

Thomas Brown, who had been a member of their society, accuses Ann Lee of being peevish, and repeatedly getting intoxicated ; and brings the latter charge also against her brother William. He says, that before 1793, " the men and women, on a variety of occasions, danced naked ;" and that twice, at least, Mother Ann, her brother, and James Whittaker, indulged in a free fight. It would perhaps be unfair to accept all the scandal which Brown chronicles. After repeated denials, however, he obtained an acknowledgment that naked dancing had been formerly practised. Flagellation was practised by the Shaker converts. A man whose daughter had thus been scourged, prosecuted the elder who had inflicted the punishment. Her sister was summoned as a witness. "She went to Whittaker, and asked him what she should say." He answered—"Speak the truth, and spare the truth; and take care not to bring the gospel into disrepute." Accordingly she testified that her sister was not naked. She was justified in giving this testimony, because her sister had a fillet on her hair!

Soon after the return from their journeyings in the eastern states, the little community lost one of its lights. We have seen that Mother Ann's husband refused to bear the Shaker cross, but her brother, William Lee, was a firm believer in his sister's mission. We are told that he was a gay young man, who had been an "officer" in the Oxford Blues. He carried to the grave the scars of wounds received in defending her, and in some respects resembled her, especially in having "visions." Like many other of the Lancashire artisans he had a good voice, which would be of service amongst those who "praise the Lord with dance and song." He died July 21st, 1784, aged forty-four years. Brown thus describes him (p. 323) "Elder William Lee seldom travelled to gain proselytes, being severe in his temper and harsh in his manners; his preaching was not fraught with that mildness and urbanity, which is necessary to draw the attention and win the affection of the hearers, and render a man beloved. It once happened, as he was speaking to a public congregation, one of the spectators, a young man, behaved with levity and disrespect; upon this, Lee took him by the throat and shook him, saying, "when I was in England, I was sergeant in the king's life-guard, and could then use my fists; but now, since I have received the gospel, I must patiently bear all abuse, and suffer my shins to be kicked by every little boy; but I will have you know that the power of God will defend our cause."

Her followers had proclaimed Mother Ann immortal, but to her also came the grim king. She died at Watervliet, on the 8th day of Sept., 1784, aged forty-eight years and six months. Whatever we may think of her peculiar religious theories, she certainly seems to have inculcated industry and benevolence by shrewd maxims, which were, however, little more than platitudes. Her piety, as shown in the Shaker book, seems to have been eminently practical. "To a sister she said, 'Be faithful to keep the Gospel; be neat and industrious; keep your family's clothes clean and decent,' &c. Further, 'Little children are innocent, and they should never be brought out of it. If brought up in simplicity they would receive good as easy as evil. Never speak to them in a passion; it will put devils into them. . . Do all your work as though you had a thousand years to live, and as though you were going to die to-morrow.'"

On the death of Mother Ann the leadership devolved upon James Whittaker, who "was freely acknowledged by the whole society as their elder." Whittaker was born at Oldham, Feb. 28th, 1751, and is thought to have been a relative of Ann Lee, as his own mother bore the same name. His parents were members of the Shaker society under Jane and James Wardley, and he was brought up under the care of Mother Ann, and was the one who is said to have succoured her when in prison, in the manner already described. Father James, as he was styled, died at the early age of thirty-seven.

In 1786, Ann Lee, the neice of the foundress, abandoned the celibate order to marry Richard Hocknell, probably a son of John Hocknell, one of the original emigrant band. Partington also left the society, but was helped by it in his declining years, notwithstanding this backsliding.

Mother Ann prophesied that James Whittaker would succeed her in the ministry, but this seems hardly to have been the case. Father James no doubt influenced the society, but it was an American convert, Joseph Meacham, who became its leader, and organised it on that basis of community of labour and property which now forms its most distinguishing feature. "His gift of Divine revelation was deeper than that of any other person, excepting Mother Ann." It was he who introduced the greater part of the "spiritualist" portion of the Shaker creed and doctrine. Meacham was succeeded by a female, Lucy Wright, but we need not farther follow the history of the sect. Its interest for us centres in its English origin.

In the New England travels of the celebrated Dr. Dwight, he gives an account of a visit, made in 1799, to the Shaker colony at New Lebanon :—"It consists," he says, "of a small number of houses, moderately well-built, and kept, both within and without doors, in a manner very creditable to the occupants. Everything about them was clean and tidy. Their church, a plain, but neat building, had a courtyard belonging to it, which was remarkably 'smooth shaven green.' Two paths led to it from a neighbouring house, both paved with marble slabs. By these, I was informed, the men enter one end of the church, and the women the other."

Their claims to miraculous powers he justly ridicules. They told him that they had restored the broken limb of a youth who then lived at Enfield, but, on enquiry, he found that the use of the limb was lost and the patient's health ruined. The Shaker *Testimony* contains several cases in which believers had received "a gift of healing." It is not necessary to detail these cases. They are not of great importance, and if we consider the curative powers of the imagination when under the influence of superstitious excitement, it will be possible to account for at least some of them without accusing the elders of the church of intentional deception.

On being present at one of their meetings for worship, Dr. Dwight was told that both words and tune were inspired. The tune was *Nancy Dawson;* and the sounds "which they made, and which they called language could not be words, because they were not articulated. One of the women replied, 'How dost thee know but that we speak the Hotmatot language? The language of the Hotmatots is said to be made up of such words.'" He challenged them to speak in Greek, Latin, or French, but they prudently kept silent.

Brown speaks thus on this topic—"Respecting such as speak in an unknown tongue, they have strong faith in this gift; and think a person greatly favoured who has the gift of tongues; and at certain times when the mind is overloaded with a fiery, strong zeal, it must have vent some way or other : their faith, or belief at the time being in this gift, and a will strikes the mind according to their faith; and then such break out in a fiery, energetic manner, and speak they know not what, as I have done several times. Part of what I spake at one time, was—' Liero devo jirankemango, ad fileabano, durem, subramo, deviranto diacerimango, jaffa vah pe cu evanegalio ; de vom grom seb crinom, as vare cremo domo.' When a person runs on in this manner of speaking for any length of time, I now thought it probable that he would strike into different languages, and give some words in each their right pronunciation : as I have heard some men of learning, who have been present, say, a few words were Hebrew, three or four of Greek, and a few Latin."

From 1785 until the close of the century, Shakerism exerted very little propagandist influence; but in 1801 came the Kentucky Revival, by which the infant church was considerably enlarged. Since then its progress has steadily, if slowly, increased, and at the present time is an object of great curiosity to outsiders.

The census of the United States supplies some meagre details respecting the Church organisation of the Shakers. In 1850 there were eleven churches, capable of accommodating 5,150 persons, and owning $39,500 of property. In 1860 there were twelve churches, which would hold 5,200 persons ; the property of the church was $41,000. In 1870 there were eighteen distinct Shaker organisations, possessing eighteen church edifices, capable of seating 8,850 persons ; the wealth of the church was $86,900.   These Shaker communities are found in Connecticut, Kentucky, Maine, Massachusetts, New York, New Hampshire, and Ohio.

The most important of the Shaker villages is that at New Lebanon.   A few passages, condensed from the account of a visit by the correspondent of an illustrated paper to this place, may be permitted :—

It is a great mistake to suppose that, like Romish monks and nuns, they shut themselves completely out of the world, and are unwilling that "publicans and sinners" should penetrate to their retreats and observe their manner of life. No people, as we can personally testify, are more hospitable, or welcome outsiders with greater apparent pleasure.   They will readily show you over their establishments ; they will freely explain to you their rules and regulations, taking care to point out the reasons for them ; and they will even admit you to their meetings and religious ceremonies.   Of course the man of the world is inclined to ridicule the grotesque postures and movements which he sees in their chapels ; but there is someting so quaint, simple, and sincere in their devotions, that even if a sense of their propriety did not check the smile or sneer, a sense of respect for their earnestness would.   At Mount Lebanon there are three separate societies within sight of each other : they are called the "North Family," "Church Family," and "Second Family."   The word "family" betrays the chief social characteristic of the sect.   Fancy a hundred men and women living together, enjoying all things, from the acres of the mutual estate, to the hats, thimbles, and books, in common : no one person owning a title of property himself, for his own particular use and enjoyment ; each labouring for all the others, and for the common weal ; working and taking pleasure in common, confessing to each other, worshipping together ! Neither do the Shakers marry, nor are they given in marriage. They live a strictly celibate life. We are told of husbands and wives who have been converted to Shakerism, who have lived for years in close married communion, and who, having entered the fold of " Believers," separate their bond, live apart each in the quarter of his or her sex, and, seeing each other every day, can only meet and converse as all the other brethren and sisters do. (See *Graphic*, 7th May, 1870.)

Shakers are fully aware of their lowly commencement. " The first in America who received the testimony of the Gospel were satisfied that it was the truth of God against all sin, and that in faithful obedience thereunto, they should find that salvation and deliverance from the power of sin for which they sincerely panted. And being made partakers of the glorious liberty of the sons of God, it was a matter of no importance with them from whence the means of their deliverance came, whether from a stable in Bethlehem or from Toad Lane in Manchester." (*Testimony*, p. 609.)

From this humble origin has sprung one of the most interesting and peculiar of the phenomena of the New World. "By their works ye shall know them." The testimony of travellers is very strongly in favour of the Shakers. They are known as an honest and industrious people throughout the States. With an entire absence of those compelling forces which ensure a modicum of work and order in the outside world, the " Believers " have greatly surpassed in peace and industry those of the outside world. " Order, temperance, frugality, worship—these," says Mr. Hepworth Dixon, "are the Shaker things which strike upon your senses first ; the peace and innocence of Eden, when contrasted with the wrack and riot of New York." They are capital agriculturalists, and have a reputation for thoroughness in all their industrial occupations. Every man has a trade ; every man and woman works with his hands for the good of the community.

The doctrine of celibacy has already been mentioned. Elder Frederick Evans, according to Mr. Dixon's report, says "that they do not hold that a celibate life is right in every place and in every society at all times; and they consider that for a male and female priesthood, such as they hold themselves to be, as respects the world, this temptation is to be put away." This is scarcely historically orthodox, or why should Ann Lee have raised her voice against the sexual law in the streets of Manchester ? The Shakers, like the Quakers, have toned down. To-day they seek no converts, but wait for the Spirit of God to bring people into their fold. They are not the fiery missioners of a century ago. They look now for increase to those cycles of religious enthusiasm which sweep over some portions of English and American society from time to time, and are known as revivals.

Their communistic views have also been named. Probationers are allowed to retain their private possessions, but the Covenanters have all things in common.

As might have been expected from their history, they firmly believe in the possibility of intercourse with the world of spirits. For them there is no death. The departed surround them in every action of life. They are living in "resurrection order," the seen and the unseen in daily communion. Ann Lee is not dead, she has merely withdrawn behind a veil, and her followers can speak with her as when she inhabited a tabernacle of flesh.

There is a charm about these mysterious people, offspring though they are of ignorance, credulity, and undisciplined enthusiasm. They have impressed many minds by their seemingly passionless existence, their abstinence and industry, and by their claims of being able to pierce that darkness which hides from us the loved and lost.

DID SHAKSPERE VISIT LANCASHIRE?

—·o◆o·—

To me it seems as if when God conceived the world, that was Poetry;
He formed it, and that was Sculpture; He coloured it, and that was
Painting; He peopled it with living beings, and that was the grand,
divine, eternal drama.—CHARLOTTE CUSHMAN.

———

MR. E. J. L. SCOTT, in a communication to the
Athenæum, No. 2830, January 21, 1882, gives a
letter from Henry le Scrope, ninth Baron Scrope of Bolton
(Yorkshire), Governor of Carlisle and Warden of the West
Marches, to William Asheby, English Ambassador at the
Court of James VI. :—

"After my verie hartie comendacions: vpon a letter
receyved from Mr. Roger Asheton, signifying vnto me that
yt was the kinges earnest desire for to have her Majesties
players for to repayer into Scotland to his grace: I dyd
furthwith dispatche a servant of my owen vnto them wheir
they were in the furthest parte of Langkeshire, whervpon
they made their returne heather to Carliell, wher they are,
and have stayed for the space of ten dayes, whereof I

thought good to gyve yow notice in respect of the great
desyre that the kyng had to have the same to come vnto
his grace; And withall to praye yow to gyve knowledg
thereof to his Majestie. So for the present, I bydd yow
right hartelie farewell. Carlisle the xxth of September, 1589.

"Your verie assured loving frend,

" H. SCROPE."

Mr. Scott continues :

"There is no further letter relating to the subject among
Asheby's correspondence, but it is very interesting to think
that Shakspeare visited Edinburgh at the very time when
the witches were tried and burned for raising the storms
that drowned Jane Kennedy, mistress of the robes to the
new queen, and imperilled the life of Anne of. Denmark
herself. In that case the witches in *Macbeth* must have had
their origin from the actual scenes witnessed by the player
so many years previously to the writing of that drama in
1606."

The editor of the *Manchester City News*, February 4,
1882, in reprinting the letter, says:—

"The letter is, however, specially worthy of note in these
columns, because it shows not only that Shakspere was in
Edinburgh at the period named (1589), but that he and his
company of players were summoned to go from Lancashire
—here spelt 'Langkeshire.'"

It may, however, be pointed out that there is other
evidence of the Queen's players having been in Lancashire.

The Queen's players came to Stratford in 1587, and this,

as Mr. Furnivall says, was probably the turning point in Shakspere's life, though Mr. Fleay holds that he must have left his native place in 1585. He is supposed to have joined this company, but we have no direct evidence of the fact, or of either of the companies called "The Queen's Players" having been James Burbage's company. The first note of Shakspere's connection with Burbage's men, who played at "The Theatre" in Shoreditch, occurs at Christmas, 1593, when, in the accounts of the Treasurer of the Chamber, his name appears after that of Kempe and before that of Burbage, in the list of "Lord Strange's servants."

The "Stanley Papers," issued by the Chetham Society, contain evidence that the company with which the name of Shakspere is traditionally associated was in Lancashire both before and after this supposed visit to Scotland. The Derby Household Book mentions the visit to the New Park in Lathom of the Queen's players on the tenth of October, 1588, and their visit to Knowsley on the 25th June, 1590, whence they departed on the following day. ("Stanley Papers," edited by F. R. Raines, pt. ii. pp. 51, 82). One would like to associate the princely house of Derby with the name and fame of our great dramatist; and there is sufficient ground for supposing that Shakspere may have visited Lancashire, though the evidence is certainly not strong enough to warrant us in asserting that he did.

THE LANCASHIRE PLOT.

Hast thou betrayed my credulous innocence
With vizor'd falsehood and base forgery?

MILTON, Comus 697.

THE town of Manchester was in a state of indignant and feverish excitement on the 17th of October, 1694, being the sixth year of the reign of William the Deliverer. Everywhere groups of townspeople were discussing the all-absorbing topic of the Lancashire plot, for on that day there came to the town four of their Majesties' judges, with every circumstance of pomp and parade, to try for their lives gentlemen of the best blood of Lancashire and Cheshire; unfortunate prisoners who were accused of having conspired against the Deliverer, of having been guilty of the treason of remaining faithful to the old king, whom the rest of the nation had cast off. The prisoners were brought into town strongly guarded, amidst the sympathetic demonstrations of their neighbours, who were equally liberal of groans and hisses for the wretched informers who were about to do their endeavour to bring them to the scaffold.

Lancashire, which in the civil war struck some hearty

blows for parliament, was now a hotbed of disaffection. The old cavalier families, in spite of bitter experience of Stuart ingratitude, remained faithful in spirit to the exile of St. Germains ; and the common people would have no love for King William, who was a foreigner, nor for Queen Mary, who sat upon the throne of her royal father, whilst he wandered a weary exile in a foreign land. The accused then would have been pretty certain of sympathy had the public mind been convinced of the reality of the supposed conspiracy. How much more so, then, when it was shrewdly suspected that the charge had been trumped up by a gang of villains eager for blood-money, and supported by greater rogues anxious for a share of the estates which would be forfeited upon the conviction of their victims? Nor was the suspicion altogether groundless, for covetous eyes were fixed longingly on these fine Lancashire acres, and the Roman Catholic gentry ran great danger of being defrauded of their inheritances.

In 1693 a commission sat at Warrington to inquire into certain lands and property alleged to have been given to " superstitious uses," *i.e.,* to ascertain whether the Roman Catholic gentry had applied any portion of their estates or income to the promotion of their faith, or the sustenance of its ministers, and if they could be convicted of this heinous crime the property was to be confiscated, and one-third portion given as the reward of the undertakers. So confident were these persons of their prey that the plunder was prospectively allotted. As the result of this commission, where the defendants were not heard, the matter was carried into the

Exchequer Chamber. Here it was pretended that at a meeting at the papal nuncio's house, Lord Molyneux, William Standish, Thomas Eccleston, William Dicconson, Sir Nicholas Sherburne, Sir W. Gerard, and Thomas Gerard, had all promised money or lands for Papish uses. But the accusers had been very clumsy, for the falsehood of each separate item of the accusation was so abundantly proved, that the Government was forced to abandon all further proceedings.

When, therefore, in the next year it was bruited about that a plot had been discovered to bring back King James and murder King William of Orange ; that men had been enlisted, commissions received from St. Germains, arms bought and concealed in the old halls of Lancashire and Cheshire, and that those who had by the Warrington inquiry been in danger of losing their broad acres, were now also likely to lose their lives ; men said, not unnaturally, that it was a base and horrible conspiracy against the Lancashire gentlemen ; and that this was the next move in the iniquitous game begun at Warrington. If broken tapsters and branded rogues were to be encouraged in devoting to the traitors' block gentlemen of rank and estate, whose life was safe ?

Such was the state of feeling amongst the crowds which surrounded the Sessions House, opposite to where the present Exchange is erected. It was not until the 20th that the trial before a jury began. On that Saturday Sir Roland Stanley, Sir Thomas Clifton, William Dicconson, Philip Langton, Esquires, and William Blundell, Gent., were placed at the bar, and, in long verbose sentences, accused both in

Latin and English, generally of being false traitors to our
Sovereign Lord and Lady, and specifically of having
accepted commissions for the raising of an army from
James the Second, late King of England. After the case
had been opened, Sir William Williams, their Majesties'
counsel, called, as first witness, John Lunt, who was asked
if he knew all the five men at the bar? Lunt, with front of
brass, answered that he did know them all. Here Sir
Roland Stanley cried out, "Which is Sir Roland Stanley?"
Whereupon, to testify how intimately the informer was
acquainted with them, he pointed out Sir Thomas Clifton!
Great was the outcry in the court, which did not lessen
when the judge bid Lunt take one of the officers' white
staves, and lay it on the head of Sir Roland Stanley, and he
again indicated the wrong man. Being asked which was
Sir Thomas Clifton he unhesitatingly pointed out Sir Roland
Stanley. Having thus shown his accuracy he was allowed
to proceed with his narrative of the plot. His evidence
asserted that in 1689 one Dr. Bromfield, a Quaker, was
sent by the Lancashire gentry to the court at St. Germains,
to request King James to send them commissions, that they
might enlist men for his service. Bromfield, being known
as a Jacobite agent, it was determined to employ some one
less known, and Lunt was pitched upon for the purpose.
So, in company with Mr. Threlfall, of Goosnargh, he came
over in a vessel which landed at Cockerham. At the residence
of Mr. Tildesley they separated and Threlfall went into Yorkshire to distribute commissions, whilst Lunt was summoned
to attend a midnight meeting of the Lancashire Jacobites,

held at the seat of Lord Molyneux, at Croxteth. Here the
persons now accused were present, and many others, none
of whom Lunt had ever seen before. The commissions
were delivered, the health drunk of their Majesties over the
water, and some little additional treason talked. At this
point in the evidence Sir Roland Stanley remarked how
improbable it was that he should accept a commission
which might endanger his life and estate from an utter
stranger. " But," cries Lunt, " I brought you with your
commission Dr. Bromfield's letter." Then the judge said
to Sir Roland, "You are answered—that was his creden-
tials ;" but did not think fit to say that Lunt had made no
mention in his depositions of this circumstance, which was
evidently invented on the spur of the moment to confound
Sir Roland Stanley. The judge also observed there was no
great matter in Lunt not being able to point out the
prisoners correctly. Lunt, thus encouraged by Sir Giles Eyre,
proceeded with his veracious narrative—swore that the Lancashire gentlemen had given him money to enlist men and
buy arms ; that he beat up sixty men in London, who were
quartered in different parts of the county palatine ; and
particularised some persons to whom arms had been sent.
In 1691 (about July or August), he was sent to France, to
acquaint the Pretender with what his friends had been
doing, and to inquire when they might expect him in
England. The spring following was named as the happy
time when the Stuarts were to be re-established on the
English throne. He also named a meeting at Dukenhalgh,
when some more commissions were distributed by Mr.

Walmsley, one of the accused.   Mr. Dicconson now asked
Lunt why he had not disclosed the existence of this terrible
plot, or why he had revealed it at all ?   Lunt was evidently
prepared for this inquiry, and his retort was prompt and
crushing.   Some proposals had been made to which he
could not assent.   Being pressed by the Court to be less
reticent, and explain his meaning, he said that there was a
design to murder King William ; that the Earl of Melfort
(the Pretender's friend and minister) had asked him to aid
in the assassination ; he had consented to do so, but a
Carthusian friar, to whom he had revealed it under confession, told him that it would be wilful murder if King
William were killed, except in open battle, and he had
revealed the plot lest his old colleagues should carry out
their wicked project.

Such, in brief, was the evidence of Lunt, deviating often
from the tenour of his previous depositions, which had been
made before he had been under the moulding influences of
Aaron Smith, an unscrupulous Jacobite hunter, whose delight
and duty it was to manage these little matters, to procure
witnesses and favourable juries.   Favourable judges were
supplied by his betters.   And to fully understand the
gravity of the prisoners' position it should be recollected
that they could not have the assistance of counsel ; their
witnesses could not be compelled to attend ; they were
ignorant of the witnesses to be produced against them ; and,
until they stood in the dock, had not heard the indictment
against them.   Every circumstance was in favour of the
crown.   Lunt's evidence was corroborated by Womball, a

carrier, and one Wilson, who had been branded for roguery, as to the delivery of commissions and arms. *Colonel* Uriah Brereton (who was, it is said, a saddler's apprentice and common sharper) testified that he had received money from Sir Roland Stanley for the service of King James. This worthy Captain Bobadil being asked if he was not poor and necessitous when he received these gifts, cried out, in true ruffler style, "Poor! That is a question to degrade a gentleman." The remaining evidence we need not go into, save that of John Knowles, who, having been sworn, declared "by fair yea and nay, he knew nout on't."

Then, after short speeches by Stanley and Dicconson, the witnesses for the defence were examined. The first half-dozen made some damaging attacks upon the character of John Lunt, representing him as a mean scoundrel, a bigamist, and a notorious highwayman. Then Lawrence Parsons, his brother-in-law, testified that he had been invited by Lunt to aid him in denouncing the Lancashire gentlemen, but had refused the offer of 20s. per week and £150 at the end, rather than "swear against his country-men that he knew nothing against." Mr. Legh Bankes, a gentleman of Gray's Inn, told how Taafe, an intimate friend of Lunt's, and who was expected to be a witness for the crown, had been to the wife of Mr. Dicconson, and revealed to her the whole design of Lunt, offering to introduce some friend of the prisoner's to Lunt, as persons likely to be serviceable in any swearing that might be needed to hang the prisoners. Mr. Bankes was suspicious of this being a trap; but having been introduced to Lunt, that worthy,

over a glass of ale, very frankly said that he wanted gentlemen of reputation to back his own evidence, and if Bankes
would join he should be well provided for. He produced
his "narrative of the plot," and Taafe read aloud this
manuscript, which named several hundreds besides the
prisoners. "Why were these not taken up also?" inquired
Bankes. Lunt's answer was, "We will do these people's
business first, and when that hath given us credit we will
run through the body of the nation." When the next
witness arose, Lunt and Aaron Smith must surely have
trembled, for it was their old friend Taafe, who, after adding
his testimony to Lunt's villainous character, gave a brief
account of that worthy gentleman's career as a discoverer of
plots. How the first one he discovered (it was in Kent)
came to nothing, as he had failed to find corroborative
evidence ; and how he was near failing again from the same
cause ; how Aaron Smith had edited and improved his
original narrative. Lunt wanted Taafe as a witness, complained that the men he had hired to swear were blockish,
and of such low caste as to carry little weight. Could Taafe
introduce him to some gentleman—(God save the mark !)—
willing to perjure his soul, consign innocent men to the
scaffold, and receive blood-money from Aaron Smith?
Taafe, from some motive not clear, determined to baulk
the villainy of his fellow-informer, hence the circumstances
narrated by Mr. Legh Bankes, whose suspicions of treachery
had prevented a full discovery. Taafe had partially opened
his mind to the Rev. Mr. Allenson, who had also distrusted
him in a similar manner. In Roger Dicconson, brother of

the prisoner, he found a bolder and more adventurous spirit. The evidence of Mr. Allenson need not be analysed. He was followed by Mr. Roger Dicconson, who told how he was introduced by Taafe to Lunt, as a proper person to aid in the plan, at a coffee-house in Fetter-lane, when they adjourned to a private room. Dicconson called himself Howard, a member of the Church of England, willing to join in the plot for a valuable consideration. Lunt said that they had gold in for £100,000 a year, and that the informants were to have a third of the forfeited estates. He asked Lunt if he knew Dicconson's brother? and Lunt, all unconscious that he was sitting face to face with him, replied, "Yes; very well, for he had delivered commissions to Hugh and Roger Dicconson about Christmas!"

Many more witnesses were examined—some of whom established that certain of the prisoners were not in the neighbourhood of Croxteth and Dukenhalgh at the time of the alleged Jacobite meetings at those places; whilst others gave most damaging evidence as to the utter rascality of Lunt and his chief witnesses — Womball, Wilson, and Brereton. The judge, in his summing up, contented himself with saying that the matter deserved great consideration, in which opinion the jury did not agree, for, after a short consultation, and without leaving court, they returned for each prisoner a verdict of NOT-GUILTY. Mr. Justice Eyres then discharged them, with an eulogy upon the merciful and easy Government under which they lived, and advised them to beware of entering into plots and conspiracies against it. Lord Molyneux, Sir William Gerard, and Bartholomew

Walmsley, Esq., were then put to the Bar, but, no witnesses appearing, they were also declared Not Guilty, which gave Mr. Justice Eyres an opportunity for another cynical speech, concluding with these words : "Let me therefore say to you, go and sin no more, lest a worse thing befall you." As they had just been pronounced innocent, the meaning and fitness of his remarks are somewhat questionable. But if his bias prejudiced him against the prisoners, they would have compensation in the popular satisfaction at their acquittal. Manchester went mad with joy. Lunt and his merry men were pelted out of the town, and only escaped lynching by the intervention of the prisoners' friends ; and all concerned in the prosecution came in for a share of popular hatred. The peril which the Lancashire gentlemen thus strangely escaped was a very great one, but the peril which the country escaped was greater still, for had there been wanting the disaffection of Taafe to his brother rascal Lunt, the courage and address of Roger Dicconson, and the honesty of the Manchester jury, England might have seen a repetition of the atrocities of Titus Oates and William Bedloe ; might have seen a bigamist highwayman going from shire to shire and fattening on the blood and ruin of the best of her nobles and gentlemen.

It is only fair to add that those who believe in the reality of the "plot" may cite the resolution of the House of Commons (who examined many witnesses on the subject some months after this trial), that there had been a dangerous . plot, and that the special assize at Manchester was justifiable. That resolution strikes one as being more political than judicial.   A prosecution for perjury against Lunt was abandoned, because it was understood that persistence in it would bring on the prosecutors the weight of the harsh penal laws.

The following books may be consulted on the subject:—Histoire de la derniére conspiration d' Angleterre [Par Jacques Abbadie], London, 1696. Jacobite Trials at Manchester in 1694.   Edited by William Beamont, 1853 (Chetham Society, vol. xxviii.).

I. Abbott's Journal; II. The Trials in Manchester 1094. Edited by Rt. Rev. Alexander Goss, D.D., 1864 (Chetham Society, vol. lxi.).

A Letter out of Lancashire to friends in London, giving some account of the late Tryals there. [By Thomas Wagstaffe], London, 1694.

Ainsworth's novel of "Beatrice Tyldesley" relates to these Jacobite Trials.

CURIOSITIES OF STREET LITERATURE.

———o◆o———

Thespis, the first professor of our art,
At country wakes sang ballads from a cart.
DRYDEN. *Prologue to Lee's Sophonisba.*

———

THE ephemeral literature of the streets—the account of a
great fire, the lamentation for some public calamity,
the apocryphal penitential verses of hardened and bloody-
minded murderers, the satirical rhymes, the tender and
amorous lay—has an interest all its own. There are few of
us but must confess to having stopped to listen to the mouldy
"patter" of the seedy-looking tatterdemalions who, keenly
alive to business, occasionally amuse a street crowd by their
voluble oratory or melancholy chant. In 1871, Reeves
and Turner, of London, published a quarto vol. entitled
"Curiosities of Street Literature." This consists of reprints
of some choice specimens of the literature by which the
flying stationers of former days made a living. From its high
price and the small number (456) printed, this work is little
known to the general public. As several of the ballads and
broadsides have a local flavour, a few words of note may not

be out of place. "The Liverpool Tragedy; Showing how
a Father and Mother Barbarously Murdered their own Son,"
is a ballad narrating the story on which Lillo founded his
play of "Fatal Curiosity." It is one of these legends dear
to the hearts of the people, which has been narrated of many
localities, and is dealt with more fully in another part of this
volume. "Th' Owdam Chap's Visit to th' Queen" (p. 66) is
in the Lancashire dialect, and written upon the occasion
of the birth of the Prince of Wales. There is one, entitled
" Peterloo," which has at least the merit of brevity :—

> See ! see ! where freedom's noblest champion stands,
> Shout ! shout ! illustrious patriot band,
> Here grateful millions their generous tribute bring
> And shouts for freedom make the welkin ring,
> While fell corruption and her hellish crew
> The blood-stained trophies gained at Peterloo.
> Soon shall fair freedom's sons their right regain,
> Soon shall all Europe join the hallowed strain
> Of Liberty and Freedom, Equal Rights and Laws.
> Heaven's choicest blessing crown this glorious cause,
> While meanly tyrants, crawling minions too,
> Tremble at their feats performed on Peterloo.
> Britons, be firm, assert your rights, be bold,
> Perish like heroes, not like slaves be sold ;
> Firm and unite let millions be free,—
> Will to your children glorious liberty ;
> While coward despots long may keep in view,
> And, silent, contemplate the deeds on Peterloo.

A more modern sample of the liberal muse is given on p.
104, "A New Song to the Memory of the late R. Cobden,
Esq., M.P." which ends—

> For ever shall his name endure,
> Tho' numbered with the dead,
> His name through earth's immortalised,—
> " He got the people bread."

" Manchester's an Altered Town" occurs at p. 122 :—

Once on a time this good old town was nothing but a village
Of husbandry and farmers too, whose time was spent in tillage :
But things are altered very much, such building now alloted is
It rivals far, and soon will leave behind, the great Metropolis.
 O dear O, Manchester's an altered town, O dear O.

Once on a time, were you inclined your weary limbs to lave, sir,
In summer's scorching heat, in the Irwell's cooling wave, sir,
You had only to go to the Old Church for the shore, sir ;
But since those days the fish have died, and now they are no more, sir.

When things do change, you ne'er do know what next is sure to follow ;
For, mark the change in Broughton now, of late 'twas but a hollow ;
For they have found it so snug, and changed its etymology,
They have clapt in it a wild beast's show, now called the Gardens of
 Zoology.

A market on Shudehill there was, and it remains there still, sir :
The Salford old bridge is taken away, and clapt a new one in, sir ;
There's Newton Lane, I now shall name, has had an alteration,
They've knocked a great part of it down to make a railway station.

There's Bolton Railway Station in Salford, give attention,
Besides many more too numerous to mention ;
Besides a new police, to put the old ones down stairs, sir,
A Mayor and Corporation to govern this old town, sir.

There's Manchester and Salford old bridge that long has stood the
 weather,
Because it was so very old they drowned it altogether ;

And Brown-street market, too, it forms part of this sonnet,
Down it must come they say, to build a borough gaol upon it.

Not long ago, if you had taken a walk through Stevenson Square, sir,
You might have seen, if you look'd, a kind of chapel there, sir,
And yet this place, some people thought, had better to come down, sir ;
And in the parson's place they put a pantaloon and clown, sir.

In former times our cotton swells were not half so mighty found, sir,
But in these modern times they everywhere abound, sir ;
With new police and watchmen, to break the peace there's none dare,
And at every step the ladies go, the policemen cry, "Move on there."

In former days this good old town was guarded from the prigs, sir,
By day by constables, by night by watchmen with Welsh wigs, sir ;
But things are altered very much, for all those who're scholars
May tell the new policemen by their numbers on their collars.

"Luke Hutton's Lamentation" (p. 165), which has been previously printed by Mr. Payne Collier, is a doleful ditty setting forth the sorrows of a highwayman who was "hanged at York" in 1598. The same fate awaited William Nevison, who is said to have performed the exploit attributed to Dick Turpin by a Manchester novelist. Nevison's ride from London to York was certainly a wonderful feat, if it ever happened at all. The ballad of "Bold Nevison the Highwayman" (p. 169) has often been reprinted. The murder of Mrs. Hutchinson at Liverpool in 1849, by John Gleeson Wilson, is set forth at page 197. The circumstances of that brutal triple murder were imprinted on many memories by their *bizarre* horror. "The Wigan Murder" (p. 203) relates the "examination and confession of John Healey."

John Healey is my name,
It was strong whisky did my head inflame,
With four companions, at their desire,
At Button Pit, near Wigan,
To thrust poor James Barton in the furnace flames of fire.

The last line, it will be seen, is, if not good measure, at least
"pressed down and running over." "The Execution of
James Clitheroe, of St. Helens" (p. 208), is a brief prose
biography of a gentleman who murdered a paralytic woman
with whom he cohabited in adulterous intercourse. "Miles
Weatherhill, the Young Weaver, and his sweetheart, Sarah
Bell" (p. 215), is a ballad story of a young man executed at
Manchester. The poet's sympathy is clearly with the crimi-
nal. He had been refused permission to see his sweetheart,
who was a servant at Todmorden Parsonage, and in revenge
made a murderous attack upon the inmates of the house.

Three innocent lives has been sacrificed,
And one serious injured all through true love.
If they'd not been parted, made broken-hearted,
Those in the grave would be living now ;

And Miles would not have died on the gallows
For slaying the maiden and Parson Plow.

*   *   *   *   *

And all good people, oh, pray consider
Where true love is planted, there let it dwell ;
And recollect the Todmorden murder,
Young Miles the weaver, and Sarah Bell.

"Trial, Character, Confession, and Behaviour of Alice Holt"
(p. 223), who was executed at Chester for the murder of her

mother.   The poor old lady appears to have died of an
insurance for £26, a not altogether novel complaint.   At
p. 2 1 3 we have a sympathetic elegy upon Allen, Gould, and
Larkin :—

> To God I recommend them, in his mercy to defend them ;
>   May their souls shine in glory upon the blessed shore.
> Safe within His keeping, where there will be no weeping,
>   Now Allen, Gould, and Larkin, alas ! are now no more.

The contents mention (p. 235) an execution paper of John
Gregson for the murder of his wife at Liverpool, but this
morceau has been cancelled and another attraction substi-
tuted in its place.   These notes may serve to show how
varied and extensive is the literature of the streets, in which
is embodied in not too flattering shape the form and pres-
sure of the time.

TURTON FAIR IN 1789.

Now he goes on, and sings of fairs and shows,
For still new fairs before his eyes arose :
How pedlars' stalls with glittering toys are laid,
The various fairings of the country maid :
Long silken laces hang upon the twine,
And rows of pins and amber bracelets shine :
How the tight lass, knives, combs, and scissors spies,
And looks on thimbles with desiring eyes :
Of lott'ries next with tuneful note he told,
Where silver spoons are won and rings of gold :
The lads and lasses trudge the street along,
And all the fair is crowded in his song :
The mountebank now heads the stage, and sells
His pills, his balsams, and his ague spells ;
Now o'er and o'er the nimble tumbler springs,
And on the rope the vent'rous maiden swings,
Capital Jack Pudding, in his party-colour'd jacket,
Tosses the glove, and jokes at every packet :
Of raree-shows he sung, and Punch's feats,
Of pockets pick'd in crowds, and various cheats.

GAY. *Shepherd's Week.*

THE village of Turton, which is associated in our minds
with memories of the pious Humphrey Chetham, the
founder, has also produced a poet who has left in halting

rhyme a record of the burning indignation which fired his soul at the enormities of Turton Fair.   The title page runs :—
" A Picturesque Description of Turton Fair, and its Pernicious consequences.   A Poem.   By William Sheldrake.

> Quo, quo, scelesti ruitis ?—*Hor.*
>
> Unhappy men ! the path in which you go,
> Will doutless terminate in endless woe.

London : Printed for the Author, and sold by B. Jackson, Bolton.   1789."   The work is dedicated to William Cross, Esq., Collector of Excise, Manchester.   "I have long thought and am happy in finding you to possess the same sentiment, 'That there are more young people debauched and undone by attending the giddy multitude in dissipation than by the open allurements of the most immoral.'"   Plunging into the "Poem," we have a description of the village of "Turton *alias* Chapel Town" :—

> *   *   *   Thirteen houses are the most
> Of which the great inhabitants can boast ;
> A little chapel too, of decent form,
> And e'en a school to make stiff youth conform.

The roads, we are told, "be narrow and knee deep in mud." The people live by agriculture and weaving, and, although generally sluggards, work hard enough for weeks before the fair in order to have money to waste.   It was the custom, we are told, of the "by-brewers" (an expressive word) tò fix the bough of a tree to their houses as a substitute for a sign. The cattle fair our poet looks upon as simply a pretext.   It is quickly over :—

So quick they're driven to the destined field,
Poor injur'd innocents compell'd to yield ;
Most cruel treatment they must needs endure,
Yet their submission makes no lashes few'r ;
And still to make these creatures smart the more,
With sharpest goads their painful flesh is tore,
Till their lank sides are mantled round with gore.

The fair seems to have commenced with a service in the chapel, after which—

* * * The pedlars cautiously prepare
Their crazy stalls on which t' expose their ware.

At midday the fun of the fair commences—

Whate'er's their lust, none needs despair to meet
With some delightful but envenomed sweet.

And the author proceeds to lament the presence of young girls at these scenes, and alludes to "the custom in this neighbourhood to court in the night." The fun and frolic, fast and furious, excites our author greatly, and he declares—

* * * 'Tis doubtless bad beyond comparing,
Unless to sottish Holcombe's curst rush-bearing ;
But, as 'twas satiris'd by an abler pen,
I'll say but little on that theme again.
Yet if reports are true, as prudence tells,
The last's unrivall'd and bears off the bells,
Because their interludes and tragic play
Are chiefly acted on the Sabbath day.
Poor soul ! how eagerly they ply their lore,
And to their tawdry garlands add one number more.

In a footnote he alludes to a poem on rush-bearing. Next

we have a picture of the rustics, inflamed by liquor, indulging in a free fight, whilst—

> *   *   *   Numerous sharpers, skill'd in wily art,
> Now on the stalls, then on the pocket dart.

A rough of the present day need not blush at the following description of his grandfather's prowess :—

> To these base men commence the dreadful fight,
> Kicking amain, and trembling with delight ;
> Nor will desist till the red current flows
> From the burst mouth, and from the flattened nose.

The poem concludes with an invocation to the "zealous few" to help him—

> Then we'll the lady of this place bequest
> To ease our minds and rid us of this pest."

Whether Mr. Sheldrake's muse was successful in mitigating the enormities of Turton Fair we know not.

LANCASHIRE BEYOND THE SEA.

Be England what she will,
With all her faults she is my country still.

CHURCHILL. *The Farewell.*

THERE is a pleasant passage in one of the books written by Elihu Burritt, "the Learned Blacksmith," wherein he speculates as to the manner in which the early American settlers gave names to the new homes they created, often in the midst of the wilderness. "A few men," he says, "with their axes, and their wives and children on ox-sleds, would venture out ten or twenty miles into the woods, and set to work building a little hamlet of log houses. Before a child was born in it this infant town must be christened and have a name. I have often wondered how they made up their minds what to call it. Perhaps there was a good deal of earnest talk among them on this point, perhaps some voting, too, with ballots made of pine or white-wood chips, with town names written on them with coal, and then dropped into the old weather-beaten round-topped hat of one of the company. Who knows how many fireside debates, adjourned from house

to house, took place before this important point was settled?
One of their number, his wife and eldest son, might have
been born in Colchester, another father or mother in Chelms-
ford, a third in Ipswich, two or three in Reading, and four
or five in Lancaster, in England. 'Which of these names
shall we give to the town we are building?' That is the
question. Can you not imagine the group gathered around
the great fire in that snow-covered cabin of logs? I fancy I
can see them now—old men with grey hair and thoughtful
faces, and strong, hard-handed men in their prime, and young
men, and boys and girls, and mothers with babies in their
arms, all sitting there in the firelight, some silently dwelling
upon sunny memories of the fatherland, while one of the
village fathers with his right finger pressed against the centre
of the palm of his left hand is trying to show why Lancaster
would be a better name than Reading. Why it should be so
it would be difficult for us to say if we had now to decide the
question. But he knows, or thinks he knows, why. See
how his nut-brown face lights up with animation as he grows
earnest in the matter. There are other faces that gleam with
the same light as he goes on with his argument. The fact is
there are more of the company born in old England's Lancaster than in Reading, and that decides the question; and
Lancaster is the name of this meek little hamlet of huts,
planted in the midst of the wild woods, and eyed suspiciously
not only by the thieving bears and growling wolves, but also
by the Red Indians, who do not like such doings on their
hunting grounds." This is, no doubt, the correct explanation
of the origin of a large number of those American names of

places that are identical with those in England. Thus there are at least 15 Readings in the United States, and 29 Lancasters in the United States and Canada. Even a casual examination of the entries in "Lippincott's Gazetteer of the World," published at Philadelphia in 1883, will show the existence of a Lancashire beyond the sea. In addition to 29 Lancasters there are 18 Prestons in the United States, and there is also Preston Bluff, Preston Cape, Preston Hollow, and Preston Lake. There is no Blackburn, but Oldham occurs in Kentucky, Texas, Arkansas, and Ohio. There is also an Oldham in Nova Scotia. Rochdale, which was formerly known as Clappville, is a post village in Massachusets. There are three Stockports in the United States. In Pendleton, West Virginia, the population in 1870 was 6,455, of whom 6,449 were American born. There are also Pendletons in the States of Kentucky, Arkansas, Indiana, Missouri, New York, Ohio, Oregon, and South Carolina. Caton in New York and Catonsville in Maryland are perhaps Lancashire reminiscences. Gorton is the name of a station in Minnesota. There is a Standish in Maine, and another in Michigan. Duxbury occurs in Massachusets and in Vermont. There is a Crompton in Rhode Island, and at least a dozen Boltons in the United States and in Canada, but our Lancashire town may not have been the prototype of them all. There are eleven Prescots in America. Burnley, in Ontario, is also known by the name of Grimshawe's Mills.

Without staying to look for further instances let us see what has been the influence in this particular fashion of the two great cities of Lancashire. In England beyond the sea there are fifteen place-names of which Liverpool forms a part. Two are in Ohio, one in Illinois, one in Indiana, one in Oregon, and one in Pennsylvania. Liverpool in the State of New York manufactures over a million bushels of salt yearly. There are two Liverpools in the Dominion of Canada; one is in New Brunswick, and the other is a town and port of entry for Nova Scotia, and is situated on the left bank of the river Mersey. Liverpool Cape is the name of a headland on the south side of the entrance to Lancaster Sound, Northern Canada, and of another headland bounding Liverpool Bay in the Arctic Ocean, immediately south-west of Cape Bathurst. Then we have Liverpool, a mountain range in East Australia; Liverpool Plains in New South Wales, and Liverpool River in North Australia.

There are forty Manchesters outside of Lancashire. There is one in California, and another in Connecticut, where they have paper mills, cotton mills, woollen factories, manufactories of silk, gingham, and stockinet; there are two in Illinois, and one in Indiana. Manchester in Iowa seems to be well provided with modern adjuncts, for though its population is only 1,566 it possesses five churches. Manchester in Kentucky is noted for its salt manufactories. There is a Manchester in Maine, and the name is borne by a popular seaside resort on the Atlantic coast of Massachusets. Close by, in the sea, is the mass of rocks known as "Norman's Woe," the name of which will be familiar to the admirers of Longfellow's "Wreck of the Hesperus." Manchester in Michigan has woollen and other industries.

Manchester in Minnesota has a population of 721. There is one Manchester in Montana, and two in New Jersey. Another tiny Manchester is situated in county Oneida, New York, and its population of 158 are provided with a church and an iron furnace. There is one Manchester in North Carolina, four in Ohio, and three in Pennsylvania. The only one in South Carolina, we regret to say, is "a decayed village." A post village in Tennessee is the home of Manchester College. There is another place bearing the name in Texas. Near Manchester in Vermont are the marble quarries of Mount Elias. There is another in Virginia, with several manufactories. There is a Manchester in Wisconsin. The most important is Manchester in New Hampshire, which stands on the Merrimac River, and is 59 miles from Boston. Its site is a plane elevated 90ft. above the surface of the river. The principal street, which is 100ft. wide, extends north and south parallel to the river. The town contains a court-house, sixteen churches, eight hotels, a Catholic orphan asylum, a convent, four national banks, five savings banks, a State reform school, a high school, and a free public library. Two daily and four weekly newspapers are published there. Manchester has several public parks, a system of waterworks which cost $600,000, and a paid fire department, with four steam fire engines. The river here falls 54 feet, and affords great hydraulic power, which is employed in manufactures of cotton and woollen goods. There are five large "corporations" which manufacture sheetings, drillings, delaines, seamless bags, &c. The capital invested in the manufactures of Manchester is about $10,000,000. There are also manufactures of steam engines, locomotives, linen goods, hosiery, paper, edge tools, carriages, shoes, soap, machinery, leather, &c. The value of the goods manufactured in a year is about $25,000,000. The population in 1850 was 13,932 ; in 1860, 20,107 ; and in 1870, 23,536.

There are three Manchesters in Canada—two are in Ontario and the third in Nova Scotia. The population of these transatlantic Manchesters is not stated in every case, but the twenty-one places about which the information is afforded contain an aggregate population of 151,110. As the narrowest limits of the original Manchester contain 341,508 it is clear that her many namesakes have not yet passed her in the race, but it must be observed that she had a considerable start of them, as the oldest cannot be much over two centuries old, whilst she was in existence nearly 2,000 years ago. It is curious that Lippincott, whilst recording such a multiplicity of Manchesters, only registers one Salford in the New World, a post village in Ontario, rejoicing in 100 inhabitants. It may be remarked that the transatlantic Manchesters and Salford do not contain as many people as the borough of Salford alone, which has now 176,233 inhabitants. No doubt in some, perhaps in many, instances these names are not direct geographical reminiscences of the Old World, but have been derived from family names. Even if these could be deducted there would still remain a considerable Lancashire beyond the sea.

MURDERS DETECTED BY DREAMS.

Murdre wol out that seene day by day.
CHAUCER. *Nonnes Preestes Tale.*

A VERY extraordinary case of a murder discovered through a dream is given in Dr. John Webster's " Discovery of Witchcraft," a book which was published in 1677. Webster, after quoting a brief notice of the case from Sir Richard Baker, says : " But we shall give it more at large as it was taken from the mouths of Thomas Haworth's Wife, her Husband being the dreamer and discoverer, and from his Son, who together with many more, who both remember and can affirm every particular thereof, the narrative was taken April the 17th, 1663, and is this :—

In the year above said, John Waters of Lower Darwen in the county of Lancaster, gardener, by reason of his calling was much absent from his family : in which his absence, his Wife (not without cause) was suspected of incontinency with one Gyles Haworth of the same town ; this Gyles Haworth and Waters Wife conspired and contrived the death of Waters in this manner.   They contracted with one Ribchester a poor man to kill this Waters.   As soon as Waters came home and went to bed, Gyles Haworth and Waters Wife conducted the hired Executioner to the said Waters, Who, seeing him so innocently laid between his two small Children in Bed, repented of his enterprize, and totally refused to kill him. Gyles Haworth, displeased with the faint-heartedness of Ribchester, takes the Axe into his own hand, and dashed out his brains : the Murderers buried him in a Cow-house, Waters being long missing the Neighbourhood asked his Wife for him ; she denied that she knew where he was.   Thereupon publick search was made for him in all pits round about, lest he should have casually fallen into any of them.   One Thomas Haworth of the said Town, Yeoman, was for many nights together, much troubled with broken sleeps and dreams of the murder ; he revealed his dreams to his Wife, but she haboured the concealment of them a long time : this Thomas Haworth had occasion to pass by the House every day where the murder was done, and did call and inquire for Waters, as often as he went near the House.   One day he went into the House to ask for him, and there was a Neighbour who said to Thomas Haworth, It's said that Waters lies under this stone, (pointing to the Hearth stone), to which Thomas Haworth replied, And I have dreamed that he is under a stone not far distant.   The Constable of the said Town being accidentally in the said House (his name is Myles Aspinal) urged Thomas Haworth to make known more at large what he had dreamed, which he related thus.   I have, (quoth he) many a time within these eight weeks (for so long was it since the murder) dreamed very restlessly, that Waters was murdered and buried under a broad stone in the Cowhouse ; I have told my troubled dreams to my Wife alone, but she refuses to let me make it known : But I am not able to conceal my dreams any longer, my sleep departs from me, I am pressed and troubled with fearful dreams which I cannot bear any longer, and they increase upon me. The Constable hearing this made search immediately upon it, and found, as he had dreamed the murdered body eight weeks buried under a flat stone in the Cow-house ; Ribchester and Gyles Haworth fled and never came again. Anne Waters (for so was Waters wifes name) being apprehended, confessed the murder, and was burned."

This is all the more notable because the narrator was neither credulous nor superstitious, but far in advance of his age.

The remarkable narrative of the Miller of Chester-le-street, may be given. It may be found in various miscellanies but is here quoted from the *Arminian Magazine* for 1785 (p. 32) :—

"About the year of our Lord 1632, near unto Chester, in the Street, there lived one Walker, a man of a good estate, who had a young woman, called Anna Walker, his kinswoman, that kept his house ; who was suspected to be with child by him. One night she was sent away with Mark Sharp, a collier, who had been born in Blackburn Hundred in Lancashire ; and was not heard of for a long time. [It was given out that she had removed into Lancashire.] In the winter, one James Graham, a miller, living two miles from the place where Walker lived, was one night very late in the mill, grinding corn.   About twelve or one o'clock, as he came down the stairs from the hopper (the mill doors being shut) there stood a woman upon the midst of the floor, with her hair about her head hanging down, and all bloody, with five large wounds on her head.   He being much affrighted, began to bless himself, and at last asked who she was, and what she wanted?   To whom she answered, " I am the spirit of such a woman, who lived with Walker; and being with child by him, he promised to send me to a private place, where I should be well looked to, until I was brought to bed, and well-recovered, and then I should come home again, and keep his house.   But, one night I was sent away with one Mark Sharp, who slew me with a pick, such as men dig coals with, giving me these five wounds, and after threw my body into a coal-pit hard by, and hid the pick under a bank.   His shoes and stockings being bloody, he endeavoured to wash them ; but seeing the blood would not wash out, he hid them there.   The apparition told the miller further, That he must be the man to reveal it, or else she must appear and haunt him.   The miller returned home, very sad and heavy, and spoke not one word of what he had seen ; but shunned, as much as he could, to stay in the mill after night, without company ; thinking thereby to escape seeing again the frightful apparition.   But one night when it began to be dark, the apparition met him again, seemed very fierce and cruel, and threatened that if he did not reveal the murder, she would continually pursue and haunt him.   Yet, for all this he concealed it, until some few nights before Christmas, when walking in his garden, she appeared again, and then so threatened him, and affrighted him, that he faithfully promised to reveal it the next morning. In the morning he went to a Magistrate, and made the whole matter known, with all the circumstances. And diligent search being made, the body was found in a coal-pit, with five wounds in the head, and the pick, shoes, and stockings, in every circumstance, as the apparition had related to the miller. On this, Walker and Sharp were both apprehended; but would confess nothing. At the assize following, viz. at Durham, they were arraigned, found guilty, condemned and executed; but would never confess the fact. There are many persons yet alive (says the relator) that can remember this strange murder, and the discovery of it: and the whole relation was printed, though now not easily to be gotten."

A modern instance may fittingly be added. The *Mirror* for June 1, 1844, contains this extraordinary narrative:— "A gentleman of veracity, the Rev. H. Alexander, lecturing at Lancaster, stated a remarkable fact which had occurred some years before. An amiable young man, named Horrocks, had been robbed and murdered. He was found with his head beaten in, apparently by bludgeons. For many months vigilant search was made for the perpetrators, but all in vain.

"One night, an individual who had been on very friendly terms with Horrocks, awoke much disturbed, and told his wife his conviction was that God had revealed to him in a vision that Samuel Longwith, of Bolton, was the murderer of his poor friend.   Longwith was a person with whom the dreamer had no acquaintance, and whom he had scarcely ever seen, and lived twenty miles off.   His wife told him to think no more about it, but to go to sleep.   He did so ; but again woke from the effects of the same dream.   He resolved to set out for Bolton instantly, and apply for a warrant against Longwith.

" He acted upon this determination ; but the magistrate to whom he applied refused to grant one upon such evidence. Passing through the market place he met Longwith, whom he immediately desired to go to a public-house with him to hear something he had to communicate.   There, locking the door, he charged Longwith with the murder.   The man was seized, and faintly denied the accusation.   In his confusion he said he was innocent, for he did not strike the blow. 'Then you know who did,' replied the friend of the mur- dered man ; and Longwith was taken up and examined.   He prevaricated in his statement, and was remanded for three days ; at the end of which, after many hours' prayer, he con- fessed that he had been induced to join three men in a robbing expedition, when, meeting Horrocks, who made some resistance, his companions murdered him.   This con- fession came out before the grand jury, and Longwith was brought to trial.   The dream was, of course, not offered in evidence ; the jury felt satisfied, and Longwith was cast.   He was doggedly silent after being found guilty, but again confessed his crime just before his execution."

According to Mr. Clegg's *Bolton Record*, Longwith was gibbeted on Dean Moor in 1796.

ROBERT TANNAHILL IN LANCASHIRE.

He could songes make, and wel endite.

CHAUCER. *Canterbury Tales: Prologue.*

THERE are probably many Lancashire men, who are familiar with the fame of the "Flower of Dunblane," and who, in imagination, have heard the cold wind blowing keenly on the "Braes of Gleniffer," who are not aware that the singer of them was for a time a workman in the busy town of Bolton.

Robert Tannahill was born at Paisley, 3rd June, 1774; he was but sickly in his early years, and the bashfulness of a lame child never forsook him in after life. His parents were not without education, and gave their children the benefit of such school instruction as they could afford. Robert did not distinguish himself except by the rhyming talent which is said to have been shown as early as his tenth year. In 1786 he was apprenticed to his father as a weaver. In 1795 he began his courtship of Jenny Tennant, the nymph who inspired the beautiful song of "Jessie the Flower of Dunblane." The "course of true love did not run smooth." Perhaps the shy poet was not a sufficiently brisk wooer for the lively and beautiful girl. It is said that Jenny Tennant, with the consent of her betrothed, went to a party with another man, and that the moody poet saw the cavalier snatch a kiss at parting. Then it was that he wrote

> But when I knew thy plighted lips
> Once to a rival's prest,
> Love-smothered independence rose
> And spurn'd thee from my breast.

The "Flower of Dunblane" married another, and her descendants in Canada and elsewhere still boast of their beautiful ancestress. The depression in trade and, perhaps, also this disappointment in love, led him to leave his native town. About the end of the year 1799, in company with his younger brother Hugh, he came to England. They came to Preston, and from thence to Bolton. They tried in vain to find work of any kind. Their small stock of cash was nearly exhausted, and they were contemplating a further tramp when they met with a cheerful individual—William Kibble—who felt a touch of sympathy for the poor young fellows. He guessed that they were Paisley weavers, told them that he had been one in the past, and offered them the hospitality of a Bolton weaver. Next morning he found work for Robert, and Hugh returned to Preston. Tannahill did not stay long in Lancashire, but in his brief stay he became a favourite with those amongst whom his lot had been cast. It is possible that we may not easily understand the position of the operatives of the Lancashire that was

then just rising to that industrial activity of which we now
see the fruits.   If sometimes it had dark days of enforced
idleness, there was another side to the picture.   Charles
Hulbert, writing of this very period, says : " Many families by
their industry, then lived happily and dressed genteelly,
perhaps much above their station.   Hair powder was worn
by every one making any pretensions to gentility, and so
prevalent was the custom that I have seen it on the heads
of well-dressed weavers, fustian cutters, tailors and shoe-
makers, and they could not be distinguished from real
gentlemen.   I remember when living at my Uncle Smiths',
about the year 1792, one Sunday evening standing with the
youth of the family near my uncle's gate, two well-dressed
gentlemen, with long watch chains, and heads loaded with
powder, commenced a rude and silly attack on my aunt's
maid, which was instantly resented by the whole party, and
a neighbour secured the fellows with an intent to deliver
them to a constable, when, demanding their names and
professions, they declared themselves to be two journeymen
calenderers from Manchester, and made a suitable apology.
This foolish custom of making their heads like cauliflowers
originated with a ballad singer in Paris, who, to obtain notice,
powdered his hair."   The two brothers were recalled to their
home by the news of their father's illness, and they arrived
in Paisley somewhere about the end of December, 1801, or
early in January, 1802.

The poet was not quite silent during his stay in England.
In 1800 he wrote a piece not improbably taken from his
own experience.

A LESSON.

Quoth gobbin Tom of Lancashire,
　To northern Jock a lowland drover,
" Thoose are foin kaise thai'rt driving there,
　They've sure been fed on English clover."
"Foin kaise ! " quoth Jock, "ye bleth'ring hash,
　Deil draw your nose as lang's a sow's !
That talk o yours is queer-like trash ;
　Foin kaise ! poor gowk ! their names are koose."
　　The very fault which I in others see,
　　Like kind or worse, perhaps, is seen in me.

There is a second piece of the same date :—

SILLER STANDS FOR SENSE.

On a Country Justice in the South.　1800.

What gars yon gentry gang wi Jock,
　An ca him Sir and Master ?
The greatest dunce, the biggest block,
　That ever Nature cuist her ;
Yet see, they've plac'd this human stock,
　Strict justice to dispense :
Which plainly shows yon meikle folk
　Think siller stands for sense.

This, says the editor, was "written by Tannahill when he resided in England, in 1800, on a country Justice of the Peace there."

The first of these is very slight, and the second, although probably representing only a passing mood of bitterness, is only one of several examples of a satirical fancy. It is not of course on such trifles that the fame of Tannahill rests, but on the fine lyrics, " Jessie the Flower o' Dunblane," the

"Braes of Gleniffer," and the "Summer Gloamin'." It was not until some years later that the shy bard was induced to send his pieces to the printer. Their popularity soon became great. "Perhaps the highest pleasure" he says, "ever I derived from these things, has been in hearing, as I walked down the pavement at night, a girl within doors rattling away at some of them." He continued a bachelor, lived a quiet, careful, saving life, but his mental strength was sapped, and his death was occasioned by his own rash act. Although he was watched by his relatives, he eluded them, and his body was found in the river on the 17th of May, 1810.

After leaving Bolton he kept up a correspondence with his good friend Kibble. Of one letter the following has been preserved :—

Paisley, 14th March, 1802.

Alek, poor Alek is gone to his long home! It was to me like an electric shock. Well, he was a good man, but his memory shall be dear, and his worth had in remembrance by all who knew him. Death, like a thief, nips off our friends, kindred, and acquaintance, one by one, till the natural chain is broken, link after link, and leaves us scarce a wish to stop behind them. My brother Hugh and I are all that now remain at home with our old mother, bending under age and frailty, and but seven years back nine of us used to sit down at dinner together (I still moralise sometimes). I cannot but remember that such things were, and those most dear to me."

In another he complains of the printers, who, owing to his poverty, refused to do anything unless he found security.

There are two interesting letters from Kibble, who, writing from Bolton, 6th April, 1807, says that he has collected in Bolton and Stockport 26 subscriptions. "I think," he adds, "you may send 30 copies, as I make little doubt but I can part with them." Writing nearly a year later, 1st March, 1808, he says, "I have interested myself in your behalf, in regard to your publication as far as my influence can extend, and have got 17 names to my list." He asks for five more proposal papers. "I intend" he says, "to send two to Stockport, as you have more acquaintances in that place at present than in this town—our dull trade being the cause of their shifting. Other two to Preston, and another for this town, which shall be in charge of Thomas Wright. I would likewise advise you," continues the kind and shrewd friend, "to enclose two or three of your songs, as I make no doubt it would turn out to your advantage." He then mentions a brother Scot who had sung one of Tanna-hill's songs "at a meeting of the Sons of Comus." Kibble testifies to the badness of trade at that time. Writing in July, he gives a lamentable explanation as to the subscription list. The money received he had given to a messenger, whose arrival at Paisley was by a very leisurely route. Indeed it seems doubtful if he ever reached there, or if Tannahill ever received any benefit from his Lancashire friends. £2 18s. were sent by this unsatisfactory emissary. Five copies of books were entrusted to a Scotch pedlar, who died of fever at Bradford, in Yorkshire. Kibble had not received a penny for these books. "The Bolton people," he says, "paid me except two copies, which it is doubtful if ever I shall receive, and two more at Stockport, which I think are safe." This was not a satisfactory report, and poor Kibble seems to have been painfully conscious of the fact. "You have ever," he says, "since our first acquaintance, possessed a very large portion of my respect and esteem, and I sincerely believe that on your part it was reciprocal, and to lose which would be to me a circumstance truly afflicting, therefore I entreat you to write. I have nothing," he continues, "new to inform you, but what is of a miserable nature; for were I to describe to you the wretched situation of the manufacturing part of this country, you would think I had ransacked the very intricacies of Pandora's box to fill up my description ; too much labour, and almost nothing for it; exceeding dear markets, and every other attendant evil fills up the cup of our misery." This is the last appearance of Kibble in the correspondence of the poet. (The extracts, &c., in this paper are from "The Poems and Songs and Correspondence of Robert Tannahill, with life and notes by David Semple, F.S.A. Paisley : Alex. Gardner, 1875." It is the fullest and most painstaking edition of the poet's works that has or probably can appear.)

Mr. James K. Waite, the courteous librarian of the Bolton Free Library, has kindly examined for me the town books and assessment books, but they contain no trace of either Tannahill or Kibble. Neither of them were house-holders of Bolton, or their holding must have been very minute. Thirty years ago the late Mr. G. J. French attempted, but unsuccessfully, to glean some particulars of the poet's stay in Bolton. Yet it is clear that it was not unpleasant, that he found work, made warm friends, and had the sympathy and the admiration of his fellow workers among the Lancashire weavers, and we may be allowed to hope that sometimes his thoughts would go back to the rough but kindly hearts he met in Bolton, even when he was wandering in his favourite locality—

Amang the brume brushes by Staneley green shaw.

POPULATION OF MANCHESTER.

Man is the nobler growth our realms supply,
And souls are ripened in our northern sky.

A. L. BARBAULD. The Invitation.

IN the reign of Henry VIII. the antiquary Leland visited
Manchester, which he described as being the "fairest,
best builded, quickest, and most populous town" of all Lancashire. This flattering character we hope it may still claim,
although its superiority will naturally be challenged by the
great seaport city of Liverpool. There were several baronial
surveys of Manchester during the middle ages, but any
deductions from them as to the number of inhabitants would
require to be very cautiously made. But we may safely say
with Mr. Harland that of the mediæval market town the
population consisted of two, or at the most three, hundred
burgesses, their families and dependants, some of whom
would be the bondmen and bondwomen of their free neighbours. Doubtless the introduction of the woollen trade,
which is supposed to have been planted in South Lancashire
by the end of the fourteenth century, would give a certain

impulse to the increase of population. In the memorable year 1588 Queen Elizabeth granted a charter to the College of Manchester, in which the population is stated to be 10,000. The later charter of Charles I. in 1635 names 20,000. In both of these cases the figures are in all probability meant to include the entire parish. In 1717 the population of Manchester was reckoned at 8,000, but even in this instance it is doubtful whether Salford is included or excluded. In 1757 a survey of the two towns showed them to contain 19,839 persons. In 1773 the matter was carefully examined into by Dr. Thomas Percival, and the results of his investigations were communicated to the Royal Society and formed the subject of some interesting comments by Benjamin Franklin. Percival's papers appeared in the "Philosophical Transactions," vols. lxiv., lxv., and lxvi. They are reprinted with Franklin's remarks in Percival's works. Bath, 1807. Vol. iv., p. 1. The later figures in this article are derived from the successive Census Reports. Percival's attempt was a veritable census, and the data obtained showed that Manchester and Salford then consisted of 4,268 tenanted and 66 empty houses, which formed the dwellings of 6,416 families, numbering in all 27,246 souls. The following details are given of the two towns :—Houses : Manchester, 3,402; Salford, 866. Families: Manchester, 5,317; Salford, 1,099. Males: Manchester, 10,548; Salford, 2,248. Females: Manchester, 11,933; Salford, 2,517. Married: Manchester, 7,724; Salford, 1,775. Widowers: Manchester, 432; Salford, 89. Widows: Manchester, 1,064; Salford, 149. Under 15 : Manchester, 7,782; Salford, 1,793.

Above 50 : Manchester, 3,252 ; Salford, 640.   Male lodgers :
Manchester, 342 ; Salford, 18.   Female lodgers : Manchester, 150; Salford, 13.   Empty houses : Manchester, 44 ;
Salford, 26.   At this time the population of Bolton was
4,568, whilst Little Bolton, "a suburb of Bolton, including
the manor and extending into the country as far as the
inhabitants are subject to suit and service," contained 771
people.   The present population of Bolton is 105,422.   The
village of Altrincham contained 1,029 people, whilst it now
has 11,249.   These and other curious particulars elicited, as
we have already mentioned, some comments from Franklin,
who, after detailing the method in which a census was understood to be taken in China, observes, "Perhaps such a
regulation is scarcely practicable with us."   Dr. Percival,
however, observed that "an enumeration of the people of
England would not be so difficult an undertaking as may at
the first view be imagined."   In 1774 an enumeration was
made of the entire parish of Manchester, and the population
was then stated at 42,937.   From 1773 to 1777 there were
built in the two towns 719 houses, of which 151 remained
uninhabited.   In 1783 there were but 6,195 houses in Manchester and Salford, and the people were supposed to be
over 39,000 in the first named, and over 50,000 in the two
combined.   At Christmas, 1788, an actual enumeration
showed that Manchester had 5,916 houses, 8,570 families,
and 42,821 persons.   In Salford there were 1,260 houses
and an estimated population of 7,566.   The people in the
two places were a little over 50,000.   From this time the
number may be said to have increased by leaps and bounds,

as will be seen from the following statement of the number of persons at each decennial period :—

	Manchester (including Ardwick, Cheetham, Chorlton, and Hulme).	Salford (including Broughton).
1801	75,275	14,477
1811	89,054	19,939
1821	126,031	26,552
1831	181,768	42,375
1841	235,162	53,200
1851	303,382	63,850
1861	338,722	102,449
1871	355,655	124,805
1881	341,508	176,233

These figures refer to the district under the control of the Town Councils of Manchester and Salford. By the reform Act of 1832 Manchester and Salford became parliamentary boroughs, and the boundaries assigned to them were not identical with the municipal limits, though those of Salford have since been made uniform. The progress of the parliamentary boroughs may be thus stated :—

	Manchester.	Salford.
1841	242,983	66,624
1851	316,213	85,108
1861	357,979	102,449
1871	383,843	124,801
1881	393,676	176,233

By the census taken in 1881 the population of the municipal borough of Manchester was returned at 341,508.

There is no reason to doubt the substantial accuracy of these figures; it would therefore appear that an actual decrease has taken place since the census of 1871, when the people in the same area numbered 351,189. A comparison of the figures will show that whilst municipal Manchester has decreased parliamentary Manchester has increased. This suggests the true explanation. There has been no real diminution, and the apparent decrease is due to the displacement of population caused by the demolition of cottage property under the powers of successive Improvements Acts, and by the gradual conversion of dwelling-houses in the central portions of the city into buildings used only for business purposes. One result has been a large influx of population into the neighbouring borough of Salford, where not fewer than 51,432 persons have been added to the inhabitants in the last ten years; that is to say, the addition made to the people of Salford in the last decade is larger than the entire population of Manchester and Salford a century ago. To ascertain the truth we must discard the arbitrary limitations indicated by local jurisdictions, for the real Manchester is the busy hive of life which extends for miles around, but has its centre in the Manchester Exchange. The two boroughs, with the urban sanitary districts immediately around them, will have a population of 800,000 persons.

The increase in rateable value is very remarkable. In 1815 the township of Manchester was rated at £308,634; Ardwick, £11,241; Cheetham, £8,651; Chorlton, £19,839; Hulme, £9,422. The townships forming the present municipal borough had therefore a total rateable value of

£357,778. The valuation for the year 1882 is £2,761,468.
The valuations of the several townships are : Manchester,
£1,803,499; Chorlton-upon-Medlock, £334,259; Hulme,
£298,676; Ardwick, £149,633; Cheetham, £154,069;
Beswick, £21,330. Beswick in 1801 had only six inhabitants, and its rateable value was nil. In 1815 Broughton
was rated at £5,082, and Salford at £49,048. The total of
£54,130 may be compared with its present assessment,
which is as follows :—Salford, £430,747; Broughton,
£167,000; Pendleton, £192,335; Pendlebury (part of),
£11,110; total, £801,192.

London is a word that may be used to indicate very
different areas. The City of London contains 6,493 houses
and 50,526 people. The city of Manchester has 77,404
houses and 393,676 population. But the metropolitan parliamentary boroughs contain 432,984 houses and 3,452,350
people, whilst the wider area embraced within the metropolitan police districts has 645,818 houses and 4,764,312
inhabitants. This greater London extends over the whole
of Middlesex and the surrounding parishes in the counties of
Sussex, Kent, Essex, and Hertford, of which any part is
within twelve miles from Charing Cross, and those also of
which any part is not more than fifteen miles in a straight
line from Charing Cross. A similar circle drawn round the
Manchester Exchange would embrace Ashton, Bolton, Bury,
Rochdale, Stockport, Heywood, Gorton, and other populous
districts, whose united population will be close upon two
million persons. Whilst greater Manchester has about two
million people, greater London has over four million inhabi-

tants.   If, however, the problem were put in another
form, it is very probable that the district for forty miles
round Manchester would be found to contain a larger number of people than any other circle of the same extent in the
United Kingdom.

In the century which has elapsed since the first attempt to
enumerate the people of Manchester and Salford the population has increased from 50,000 to 569,000 persons.   A
hundred years has sufficed to transform the already prosperous
market town into a metropolitan centre of enormous propor-
tions and the seat of an industry of world-wide importance.

PRINCE CHARLES EDWARD STUART'S SUPPOSED
VISIT TO MANCHESTER.

His fair large front and eye sublime declared
Absolute rule ; and hyacinthine locks
Round from his party forelock manly hung
Clustering, but not beneath, his shoulders broad.

MILTON. Paradise Lost.

DID the young Pretender visit Manchester in 1744? There is a curious Manchester tradition that "bonnie Prince Charlie" visited Manchester in disguise in 1744. The statement first appeared in Aston's "Metrical Records of Manchester." :—

In the year Forty-four a Royal Visitor came—
Tho' few knew the Prince, or his rank, or his name—
To sound the opinions, and gather the strength
Of the party of Stuart, his house, ere the length,
Then in petto, to which he aspired,
If he found the High Tories sufficient inspired
With notions of right indefeasive, divine,
In favour of his Royal Sire and his line.
No doubt he was promised an army ! a host !
Tho' he found, to his cost, it was a vain boast :

For when he returned, in the year Forty-five,
For the Crown of his Fathers, in person to strive,
When in Scottish costume, at the head of the clans,
He marched to Mancunium to perfect his plans,
The hope he had cherished from promises made
Remains to this day as a debt that's unpaid.

In a foot-note to this passage, the doggerel chronicler states that " Charles Edward Stuart, commonly called the Young Pretender, to distinguish him from his father, then alive, calling himself James the 3rd, visited Sir Oswald Mosley, Bart., of Ancoats Hall, in the year 1744, and remained with him for several weeks : no doubt with a view to see the inhabitants of Manchester and its vicinity who were attached to the interests of his family."

The improbability of Prince Charles venturing into England in disguise at the period named is so great, that very conclusive evidence should be adduced in support of the statement if it is to receive general credence. The first thought is, that if the event really took place, some memorial of it would most probably be preserved among the archives of the Mosley family. On turning to Sir Oswald Mosley's very interesting history of his family, we find the incident duly recorded : not however, on the authority of the family, but, as will be seen from the following extract, from a less reliable source :—

"In the year 1815, a very worthy and intelligent woman died in Manchester at the advanced age of eighty-four years . . . . . the following anecdote she had often, during the course of thirty years' acquaintance, repeated with the most minute exactness to Mr. Aston . . . . who kindly communicated it to me. When she was a girl of thirteen, her father, whose name was Bradbury, kept the principal inn at Manchester. It occupied the site of a house lately known by the sign of the Swan, in Market Street; and at that time was the only place where a postchaise was kept, or the London newspapers regularly received, which were brought by post only three times during the week. In the summer of the year before the Rebellion, or, as she used to say, before the Highlanders arrived from Scotland, a handsome young gentleman came every post-day for several weeks in succession from Ancoats Hall, the seat of Sir Oswald Mosley, where he was on a visit, to her father's house to read the newspapers. He appeared to hold no communication with any one else, but to take great interest in the perusal of the London news. She saw him frequently, and could not help admiring his handsome countenance and genteel deportment; but she particularly recollected that, on the last day that he came to her father's house, he asked for a basin of water and a towel, which she herself brought up, and that after he had washed himself he gave her half-a-crown. . . . . In the following year, when the rebel army marched into the town, as she stood with her father at the inn door, the young prince passed by on foot at the head of his troops; and she immediately exclaimed, 'Father! father! that is the gentleman who gave me the half-crown.' Upon which her father drove her back into the house, and with severe threats desired her never to mention that circumstance again, which threats he frequently repeated, after the retreat of the Scotch army, if ever she divulged the secret to any one." ("Family Memoirs," by

Sir Oswald Mosley, Baronet.   Printed for private circulation, 1849, p. 45.)

In after years, however, she stated that her father himself owned to her that the handsome young stranger and the unfortunate prince were the same person.

Such then is the very slender foundation upon which the legend is based.   In Byrom's " Diary " there is an unfortunate hiatus; no entry .is made in the year of the Pretender's supposed visit; but to make up for this, we have a very graphic diary, kept by Miss " Beppy " Byrom, of events during the Rebellion; and, amongst other incidents narrated by this lady, we have a very vivid picture of an interview between the prince and the celebrated John Byrom, M.A., F.R.S., and some other inhabitants of Manchester who were shrewdly suspected of bearing no great love to the House of Hanover.   If the young Chevalier had really been in Manchester the year before, he would surely have made some allusion to that event, which was one of a romantic nature, and likely to have impressed itself upon the fair Jacobite whose diary we now quote :—

"[November] Saturday 30th, St. Andrew's day.   More crosses making till twelve o'clock : then I dressed me up in my white gown, and went up to my aunt Brearcliffe's, and an officer called on us to go and see the Prince ; we went to Mr. Fletcher's and saw him get a-horseback, and a noble sight it is, I would not have missed it for a great deal of money.   His horse had stood an hour in the court without stirring, and as soon as he got on he began a dancing and capering as if he was received with as much joy and shouting almost as if he had been King without any dispute : indeed, I think scarce anybody that saw him could dispute it. As soon as he was gone, the officer and us went to prayers at the old church at two o'clock by their orders, or else there has been none since they came. Mr. Shrigley read prayers ; he prayed for the King and the Prince of Wales, and named no names. Then we all called at our house and eat a queen-cake and a glass of wine, for we got no dinner ; then the officer went with us all to the Camp Field to see the Artillery. Called at my uncle's, and then went up to Mr. Fletcher's ; stayed there till the Prince was at supper, then the officer introduced us into the room ; stayed awhile, and then went into the great parlour where the officers were dining ; sat by Mrs. Starkey ; they were all exceeding civil, and almost made us fuddled with drinking the P. health, for we had no dinner ; we sat there till Secretary Murray came to let us know that the P. was at leisure and had done supper, so we were all introduced, and had the honour to kiss his hand ; my papa was fetched prisoner to do the same, as was Dr. Deacon. Mr. Cattell and Mr. Clayton did it without ; the latter said grace for him. Then we went out and drank his health in the other room, and so to Mr. Fletcher's, where my mamma waited for us (my uncle was gone to pay his land-tax), and then went home."

There is not the slightest hint in this of the prince's previous visit ; yet these were the leading Jacobites in Manchester, and, if any persons could have aided the prince's errand in 1744, they were undoubtedly Byrom, Clayton, and Deacon. If we add to this the fact, that no other evidence has come to light of this excursion to England, that all historians and biographers have preserved complete silence on the subject, and when we also consider the foolishness, futility, and useless danger of such an enterprise, we shall be quite warranted in discrediting the Manchester tradition ; at least, until corroborative evidence of some sort is produced.   Another point of difficulty is, why the town of Manchester *alone* should have been honoured with this visit.   True, it was supposed to have Jacobite tendencies ; but the Scotch were known to be still more devoted to the old family, and no one pretends that "bonnie Prince Charlie" visited any of his Highland friends in the year before the rebellion.   The late Mr. B. B. Woodward examined for me the Stuart Papers in the Royal Library at Windsor Castle, but they did not definitely show the whereabouts of Charles Edward Stuart during the summer preceeding the Rebellion.

. It may, perhaps, not be inappropriate to transcribe a song relating to—

THE MANCHESTER REBELS.

A New Song.

To the Tune of 'The Abbot of Canterbury,'

You have all heard, no doubt, of the Devil at Lincoln,
A strange and a terrible Matter to Think on ;
But listen awhile, and I'll lay before ye
By far a more strange, aye—and wonderful Story.
        Derry down, down, &c.

We Manchester Men are so stout, or so righteous,
It is not one Demon or two that could fright Us ;

But where is the Man—If wrong, set me right in't—
That can face a whole Legion without being frighten'd?

That *Lucifer's* Agents here swarm in the Street,
You need only ask the first *Non-Con* you meet:
He'll swear are such Crowds, and they make such a Riot,
That Folk cannot go to the *Meeting* in Quiet.

What Marks they are known by—'tis fit to declare,
For the Use of the Publick—and now you shall hear:
Imprimis, their Looks—a Thing very essential,
Are drest up with nothing but *Smiles complacential*.

And as for their Garb—It is not of that Hue
Which your common Fiends wear, but Red, Yellow, and Blue,
Work'd up with such Art as to drive us all mad—
In short, my good Friends, 'tis an arrant *Scotch* Plad.

But what's worst of all, and what chiefly perplexes
Us here is, in Truth, we have Fiends of both sexes:
Here struts the Plad Waistcoat—there sails the Plad Gown,
Such fashions infernal sure never were known.

There's one Thing besides you must know, by the bye,
To add to our Plagues, there's a numerous Fry
Of young Rebel Imps—little Impudent Things,
With ' God bless P. C.' on their *Pincushion Strings*.

Now God keep us all from this Infidel Race,
Or send to support us a little more Grace:
May all Jacobite Knaves be truss'd up in a Lump,
That dare, for the future, shout *Down with the Rump*.
                    Derry down, &c.

(*A Collection of Political Tracts.* Edinburgh: printed
in the year 1747, p. 34,)

CONGREGATIONALISM AT FARNWORTH,
NEAR BOLTON.

No silver saints by dying misers giv'n,
Here bribed the rage of ill-requited heav'n :
But such plain roofs as Piety could raise,
And only vocal with the Maker's praise.

POPE. *Eloisa to Abelard.*

MR. SIMEON DYSON, in a small volume issued by
Messrs. Tubbs, Brook, & Chrystal in 1881, gives, in
a very unpretending style, some interesting particulars as to
the growth of "Rural Congregationalism in Farnworth."
The first place of worship in the village was an Independent
Chapel founded in 1808. An attempt was first made to
provide a place where Nonconformists might hold alternate
services, but the effort was not successful. After one or
two preachers, whose tenure was of a temporary nature, Mr.
Joseph Dyson walked on Saturday from Marsden, near
Huddersfield, preached three times on the Sunday, and walked
back again on Monday morning. In 1813 he became the
regular minister of this congregation, most of whose members

were in a "humble sphere of life," and some "rather in indigent circumstances," but who were anxious to have a settled preacher among them. At the ordination twenty ministers were present, and the cost of providing dinner for them and for the leading members of the congregation did not amount to £3. After a time there was added a minister's house and a Sunday school. One of the "teachers" began the task of instruction when his acquaintance with the alphabet did not extend beyond the letter O! The constable was in the habit of pushing into the chapel any loiterers whom he encountered, and the author tells us that he has himself seen the birds popping their heads out of the pockets of the pigeon-flyers thus forcibly brought to hear the gospel. The chapel had no warming apparatus, and the women not unfrequently brought with them a warm brick, which was wrapped up in a shawl, and thus made a cozy footstool. Some of the congregation came from a distance in market carts, and one, a crippled schoolmistress, was brought to chapel in a wheelbarrow. There were no organs used in those days, but "the band on the occasion of the Sunday School Anniversary Sermons generally consisted of six or eight violins, a viola, two or three violoncellos, one double bass, two or three clarionets, two flutes, two bassoons, a large brass serpent and one trombone." The Rev. William Jones, after the performance of the "Hailstorm Chorus," from Handel's Oratorio of "Israel in Egypt," grumpily observed, " Now I will try to preach to you after this furious storm." In 1831 the first "treat" to Sunday scholars was given, but was of a very modest character. The first "tea party" was held on the day of the coronation of William IV., and the task of feeding the 400 who came to it taxed the ingenuity of the ladies, and emptied all the provision shops of the neighbourhood. The Sunday evening lectures given by Mr. Dyson were sufficiently quaint in their titles, "New Cart" and "A Man Better than a Sheep" may be cited. He continued as a pastor until 1855, when increasing infirmities led to his resignation. The old chapel was left for a more modern building, and converted into a Sunday school. Mr. Dyson's jubilee was celebrated in 1863. He died in 1867, and his funeral was conducted by one of the ministers who had ordained him fifty-four years

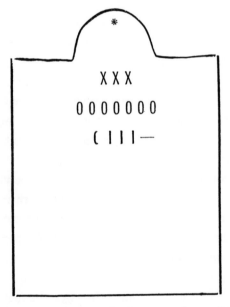

earlier. Some amusing particulars are given of the customs and mode of living seventy years ago. The "badger's" mode of reckoning is explained. Thus 0 stood for a shilling, x for 10s., and a straight stroke for a penny, and a horizontal line indicated a half-penny. Each customer had a separate board on which his cabalistic indebtedness was inscribed. This board would indicate an indebtedness of £1 17s. 9½d. A newspaper was jointly subscribed for by several of the more important inhabitants, and was solemnly passed from house to house. The Halshaw Moor Wakes were the scene of bull-baiting, badger-baiting, grinning through a horse collar and other rude sports. The inhabitants, however, if unlettered, were honest and kindly, and had a native shrewdness and a determined love of joking which compensated in some measure for the hardness of their lot.

It may be added that this village is sometimes named as the birth place of Abp. Bancroft. The prelate himself states that he was born at Farnworth, in Lancashire, and it has generally been assumed that the important manufacturing district of Farnworth, near Bolton, was meant. Canon Raines thought that Farnworth, near Prescot, was the place, and a writer in the *Bolton Journal*, in 1877, made some inquiries, and in the Prescot registers found under September, 1544, the entry of " Ric. Bancroft, sone unto John Bancroft, bapt. the xii. day." (See also Notes and Queries, 5th S. vii. 84.)

THE ESTATES OF SIR ANDREW CHADWICK.

The mould of a man's fortune is in his own hands.

BACON. *Essay on Fortune.*

NEWSPAPER readers will remember that from time to time the faithful chroniclers of the day have recorded the appearance of one or more claimants to the fabulous wealth supposed to be waiting for the heirs-at-law of Sir Andrew Chadwick. With some persons of the same family name as the knight the existence of this vast property and of their right to it became a fixed idea. English and American Chadwicks alike believed themselves entitled to sundry millions. A " Chadwick Association " formed in the State of New York sent an agent to this country ˈto investigate the matter, and a similar English Society has also been at work. The latter society had its headquarters in Manchester, and issued an elaborate report, in which the entire question is discussed with great ability and honesty. The ability is shown by the fulness of the information which has been gathered and the honesty by the unpalatable advice given to the claimants, who are warned that they are upon a hopeless quest. (Reports on the estate of Sir Andrew Chadwick and the recent proceedings of the Chadwick Association in reference thereto, by Edmund Chadwick, chairman, and James Boardman, secretary and treasurer. To which is prefixed the life and history of Sir Andrew Chadwick, by John Oldfield Chadwick, F.S.S., F.R.G.S. London : Simpkin, Marshall, and Co.)

The Chadwicks have been known in Lancashire for many centuries. A branch of the family of yeoman standing appear as owners of Carter Place, near Haslingden, a property which they held by a copyhold tenure from the Duke of Albemarle. Ellis Chadwick in 1580 was admitted to this property, and in 1603 the name of his son Robert is entered on the court rolls. The son of Robert was another Ellis who was admitted in 1684, and was then described as " gentleman," and resident in Dublin. Sir Andrew, his son, was entered on the rolls in 1726. It is therefore evident that the Haslingden yeoman's son left his fatherland to settle in Dublin. That some amount of success attended his efforts may be conjectured by the higher social appellation given to him at a time when etiquette was more rigorous in such matters than it is at present. Andrew Chadwick is believed to have been born in Dublin about 1683, but the certificate of his birth or baptism has been sought for in vain. Absolutely nothing is known as to his father's marriage, and an apparently groundless suspicion has been raised as to his legitimacy. Ellis Chadwick died in 1687 or 1688, when he would not be more than 23 or 24 years old. Of the early life of his son there is nothing certainly known, but his youthful experiences had left a bitter taste, for in a codicil to his will, written twelve days before his death, and when he was probably in his 84th year, he speaks of the "base and cruel usage he met with from his relations when he was an orphan." Notwithstanding, he desired £10,000 to be divided amongst those who could prove their consanguinity. Seven days later he revoked this bequest to those whom he describes "as the hungry Lancashire kites to whom I owe nothing either by the ties of blood, gratitude, or natural affection." This revocation is made lest they, he continues, "may attempt to run away with more, contrary to my inclination, than they deserve at my hands or can make good use of." Nothing is known as to the nature of this cruel usage, and the next record we have of the Anglo-Irish boy, left an orphan in his childhood, is that he was knighted by Queen Anne on the 18th of January, 1709-10. Why he received this honour is a mystery. He was one of the Band of Gentleman-Pensioners, but did not apparently enter that corporation until about the period of his knighthood. He was married 14th November, 1718, to Margaret Humfrey, the daughter of a well-to-do apothecary. Lady Chadwick survived her husband, and after his death had reason to suspect that he had improperly converted to his own use some property which rightly belonged to her and her sister. The marriage was without issue, but Sir Andrew is conjectured to have had a natural daughter, to whom he left a legacy of £5,000.

How he acquired his fortune is almost as mysterious as the
other parts of his life. In addition to the agency of several
regiments he was paymaster of a troop of Horse Guards,
and paymaster of a lottery office in the Exchequer. These
were doubtless lucrative appointments, but he was also
engaged in other business, the nature of which is not known.
Between 1717 and 1735 he acquired property in the neighbourhood of Golden Square, Westminster. His only
recorded visit to Lancashire was in 1726, when he attended
the halmot court at Haslingden. In 1719 he had been
summoned as a witness in the Duchy Court of Lancaster,
but had ignored the subpœna and the subsequent warrant
for his arrest, which only ran in the County Palatine. He
lived in the latter part of his life at No. 12, Broad-street,
employing four servants, each of whom received an annuity.
His silver plate weighed 2,378 ounces. In 1765 he made
a will, which was informal as to real estate because not
witnessed. This he secreted. To the will were added no
less than seven codicils—the last written within three days
of his death, which occurred 15th March, 1768. These
documents contain a number of legacies. John Wilkes is
named in one as legatee for a few thousand pounds. A few
days later this is revoked. Another patriot of the period
appears to have had much influence with Sir Andrew. This
was a pamphleteer, named Alexander Scott, who is
designated in the will to receive £500. By the first codicil
this is increased to £1,000, and by the sixth to £2,000,
and the whole residue of his real and personal estate. The
will also prohibited Lady Chadwick from continuing her

friendship with a Mrs. Glover, whose volubility appears to have offended the eccentric knight. Scott first consented to absolve the widow from the penalties attached to the continuance of this intimacy, but immediately afterwards began a Chancery suit with the object of stripping her of all interest in the residue of the estate. She died in 1783 before the conclusion of the suit, which was eventually decided in her favour. The personal estate of Sir Andrew, amounting to more than £20,000, was thus disposed of in legacies and in law expenses. The amount of the residue which was received by Scott is not known. Chadwick's will was not sufficiently formal to apply to real estate, but a claimant speedily appeared in the person of Sarah Law, the daughter of his uncle Robert, and she succeeded in satisfying the court, and was invested with the freeholds. Yet at this time there was one nearer in blood alive, in the person of Joseph, the son of James, the eldest of the uncles of Sir Andrew. Some doubt has been thrown on the marriage of this James, but its validity was accepted in a later litigation. Moreover, there was some doubt as to the legitimacy of Sarah Law. That lady, even when in possession, seems to have had some doubt as to her tenure, and conveyed the property to her son-in-law, John Taylor, a blacksmith, of Bury. The representatives of a disinherited son vainly endeavoured to upset the deed of gift. Taylor made an arrangement with Lady Chadwick for the commutation of her dower, and the whole of the freehold property gradually passed by sale and bargain into other hands. Sarah Law died in 1791, and her will confirmed the previous deed of gift. The copyhold property at Haslingden was also adjudged to Sarah Law notwithstanding the objection of her cousin Mary Duckworth, and has since by sale passed into other hands. The free leaseholds were held to be personal property, and passed to Scott. Some other leaseholds were held in trust in the names of Horsey and Campion. Sarah Law could not secure possession, as the leases did not run out until 1847, and no claim was then preferred by her representatives. In 1840 Mr. John Chadwick, of Westleigh, presented a petition to the Court of Chancery, setting forth his descent from James, the eldest uncle of Sir Andrew. After investigation he was decided to have established his claim, and the leasehold property was secured to him by a judgment of the court. Some of the statements made in the present report tend to invalidate his claim; but an attempt to eject him in 1859 proved a failure, and an uninterrupted possession of more than 30 years is a sufficient bar to any future attempt of the same kind. There is, therefore, at the present moment no property left by Sir Andrew Chadwick which has not been adjudged by the law, with the exception of £100, with interest accumulating at the rate of 3 per cent, registered at the Bank of England in July, 1768, in the names of Sir Andrew and of the Rev. Samuel Grove. This could only be claimed by joint representatives of Scott and Grove, as it formed part of the personal estate, and as such followed the dispositions of the will. The numerous Chadwick claimants of the present day are, therefore, in search of a mere chimera. There is no Chadwick estate capable of any further legal distribution.

We have said that some doubt has arisen as to the title of
the late Mr. John Chadwick, of Westleigh. He descends
from James, the eldest uncle, about whose marriage there is
some doubt.   The grandson Thomas was twice married,
and a descendant of this first marriage is now in practice as
an engineer.   The Westleigh claimant is the issue of a
second marriage, and is, therefore, remoter in blood.   In
addition to this disqualifying circumstance the second union
of Thomas Chadwick was one of doubtful validity.   He
married Betty Hopwood, a " widow," whose husband, like
Enoch Arden, turned up unexpectedly some years after he
was supposed to have shuffled off this mortal coil.   In 1859
the descendant of a younger brother of Thomas Chadwick
attempted to gain possession of the lands held by Chadwick,
of Westleigh.   This was unsuccessful on the ground that
the claim was barred by the statute of limitations, and that
even if there had been any fraud it might have been discovered earlier by due diligence.   Another claimant
appeared in 1861, but his pedigree was declared by Vice
Chancellor Wood to be imaginary.   Chadwick, of Westleigh, was only able to obtain possession of eleven houses
valued at £10,000.   He then commenced an action against
Messrs. Broadwood, of the Golden Square Brewery, which
formed part of the old knight's property.   But the
defendants, having an affidavit from David Hopwood, half
brother of the claimant, as to the bigamous marriage, defied
him to proceed, and in effect he abandoned his claim.   In
1851 John Stanton, who appeared as a descendant and
representative of Sarah Law, filed a bill against Chadwick,

of Westleigh, which contained allegations of fraud in respect of the same event. Mr. Chadwick, in 1855, purchased from Stanton "all his estate and interest" in the property which had formed the bone of contention. Mr. Chadwick died in 1861, and thus left his heirs a two-fold title, one by purchase from the representative of Sarah Law, who a century earlier had been declared the heir-at-law, and the other by the finding of 1842, that *he* was the heir-at-law. No case of this kind would be complete without a mutilated register, and accordingly a charge was brought that the leaf containing the marriage record had been cut out. This charge was declared to be baseless by the court.

Seeing that all the Chadwick property can be accounted for it is somewhat difficult to imagine how the fables as to its vast extent and unclaimed condition arose. Instead of 53 houses in the Golden Square district Sir Andrew has been credited with the possession of 1,009 houses, comprising an entire quarter in one of the richest parts of the metropolis. To this were added the manor of Hampstead, the forfeited estates of the Derwentwaters, and some square miles of county Wicklow, "with rich soil above, and gold mines beneath." Still more preposterous are the statements circulated amongst the American claimants.

It is possible that the fight over the personalty of Sir Andrew may have called attention to the existence of an urban property awaiting an heir-at-law. In 1766 Edward Birch and Matthew Martin came into possession of a draft will made by Sir Andrew in 1764. This suggested to them a plot for the forgery of a will disposing of the property to some supposed near relatives in Ireland. The fraud was discovered, and, on their trial, Whatman, the paper manu-facturer, testified that the will dated in 1764 was written upon paper which he had made himself in 1768. They were hung 2nd January, 1772. This tragic case would give still further notoriety to the Chadwick property.

The complications of the great Chadwick claim are fully shown in the report already mentioned. Mr. J. Oldfield Chadwick has made the most of the scanty materials for a biography of Sir Andrew. The chairman and secretary of the Chadwick Association have shown both wisdom and courage in advising the abandonment of any further attempt at litigation. The case was submitted to Mr. W. W. Karslake, Q.C., who not only holds that any attempt to disturb the present possessors would be unavailing, but evidently inclines to the opinion that the " Chadwick Association " might be charged with the offence known as " maintenance." As early as 1836 there was a club for the purpose of getting up a case. Later there was a com-bination to oust Chadwick, of Westleigh, with the under-standing that if successful the spoils should he divided amongst the victors. Sir Andrew Chadwick had no kindly feelings towards his relatives, and rarely mentioned them without maledictions. A superstitious mind might see the accomplishment of these curses in the unhappy fate of more than one of the claimants. Perseverance which would have commanded success in the ordinary business of life has been devoted to this lost cause, and has only ended in disappointment and the workhouse.

MANCHESTER IN 1791.

What's past is prologue.

SHAKSPERE.

THE march of change is so rapid that we are almost as far removed from the world of 1791 as from the era of Elizabeth. In that year the battle of the Nile had not been fought, America was a nation only nine years old, France was occupied in trying Louis XVI. for high treason, Napoleon was yet an unknown man, Pitt and Fox were in the height of their reputation, Wilberforce was struggling for the freedom of the negro, and Burke declaiming against Warren Hastings. Cowper, the wreck of his former self, was living in 1791, and the grass was hardly green over the graves of Johnson and Goldsmith.

The factory system was unknown; power looms had been introduced into Manchester the year previously but had proved a failure. Market-street was a narrow little thoroughfare thronged to excess if a man and a cart attempted to go down it together: the pillory still stood in the Market-place, and the scold's bridle was in frequent requisition. Manches-

ter was already beginning to make itself heard in the political
world, and boasted of a "Constitutional Society," which
made more noise than any other association in the land.   Of
this club Dr. Thomas Cooper was the leading spirit; he
afterwards emigrated to America, and died full of years and
honours in the land of his adoption.   Railways, telegraphs,
and penny newspapers were unknown, and finally in that
year was published a little book whose title is here copied:—
"A Poetical Satire on the Times."   London : Printed for the
Author, in the year 1791.   8vo., pp. 80.

The collector who found this amongst the literary lumber
of a second-hand book shop would expect to find praise or
denunciation of heaven-born ministers, and jokes about
Fox's passion for gambling, and Selwyn's fondness for execu-
tions, but his attention would be arrested by these words :

> In a fair town where commerce does abound,
> And wealthy manufacturers are found ;
> Whose gallant sons withstood the dreadful shock
> Of combined foes on Gibraltar rock.

The "poem" is really a curious satire on the Manchester
men and manners in 1791.

The Warden of the Collegiate Church is thus neatly por-
trayed :—

> At the corner of old Millgate if you stop,
> You'll see his likeness in the picture shop ;
> When for charity the beggarman apply'd,
> Charity begins at home, the D[octo]r cry'd !

This is an allusion, probably, to Tim Bobbin's caricature of the Pluralist and the old Soldier, referred to elsewhere in this volume.

Some others of the clergy come in for a share of abuse; but the writer shows that his denunciations are not the result of blind hatred, by giving this emphatic testimony to the work of the saintly John Clowes, a man who might have passed as the original of Bunyan's Evangelist, had he lived a century earlier.

> Near St. J[ohn]s Church too you may find,
> One gentle, good, beneficent, and kind,
> Brought up in strict discipline's rigid rules
> And master of the language of the schools:
> 'Cause he preaches Christ with energy divine,
> Some say he to the Methodists incline;
> Each day you pass his house you're very sure,
> To see the welcome beggar at his door;
> Thro' charity he acts and not for fame,
> O ! did our learned prelates do the same.

The Manchester Nonconformists, he tells us, are

> A people which, if they are not bely'd,
> Are not so fond of Christ as they're of pride.

From the parsons to the lawyers, and from the lawyers to the doctors, our satirist proceeds with rapid strides, and is loud in complaints about the management of the Infirmary, and various other matters.

Then he spreads his wings for a more adventurous flight, and dilates on the excellencies of Dryden, Pope, Goldsmith, Thomson, &c.

After this moderate digression he returns to

> View Mancunium, the town of fame,
> And see if it can own a poet's name ;
> The British Lion, when put into ire,
> Has rous'd great Neptune, set the seas on fire.

(Fortunately there was enough water left to extinguish this novel conflagration.)

There is an old story of an Italian malefactor who was allowed to choose whether he would serve as a galley slave or *read through* the ponderous History of Guicciardini. He selected the book, but after three months hard labour at it, he returned to his judges with an earnest and piteous request to be sent to the galleys. Had this convict been offered the alternative of reading the productions of Poet Ogden, he would not have had the courage to attempt their perusal. He would have run away from the " British Lion Rous'd," have seen no archness in " Archery," no " Paradise Lost " in " Emanuel," and whould have hoped for a General Deluge to carry them all away. Guicciardini would beat Ogden in size, but for leaden weight, this Manchester bard may be backed against all the tribe of Parnassus. No ship could hope to near port in safety if Ogden's poems by accident got amongst the ballast.

From the poet to the players is an easy transition, and so our hobbling rhymester exclaims :—

> Did I a playhouse mention with your pardons?
> The house alluded to is near S[prin]g G[arde]ns,
> Their merits should not make we Christians fret,
> But Philodramatic says they're no great set,
> The manager's huge form may please beholders,
> Like Great Goliath with Herculean shoulders.

Then addressing the players, our censor with a frown proceeds to take them to task, and sternly asks—

> Do you think, my friends, you never make mistakes?
> Does each man fill the post he undertakes?
> To be a player you know requires skill,
> You are all players if we believe the bill,
> But one does emulate his namesake king,
> He speaks distinctly, makes the house to ring,
> Mr. K——— does with much judgment play his part,
> He needs no prompting, has it all by heart ;
> He is genteel and has a comely face,
> The heroines of our stage I can't traduce,

[Is this an admission that he has traduced the heroes of the stage ?]

> To run down females would be rank abuse ;
> A general actress in this house we see,
> The oft-applauded lady, Mistress T.
> In Tragedy, great ; in Comedy, no less—
> Plays Widow Brady always with success.

This, one feels, is the highest stroke of success. To be "great" in Tragedy is much, to be equally great in Comedy is more ; but what are the qualifications necessary for such trivial successes when compared with the amazing genius— the concentrated gifts required for the successful delineator of Widow Brady. Some of our satirist's effusions are very obscure, some of them are very personal, and some of them are slightly indecent. For these reasons our quotations are necessarily few.

ORIGIN OF THE WORD "TEETOTAL."

Suiting the action to the word, the word to the action.

SHAKSPERE.

IN the year 1882 the "Temperance Jubilee" was generally celebrated, but in assigning the year 1832 as the origin of the movement for total abstinence from intoxicants it must not be supposed that there were no water drinkers before Joseph Livesey. In every age there have been individuals who, with or without "pledge," have abstained from intoxicants. There were, it is said, in ancient Egypt persons who were bound by oath not to drink of wine; whilst amongst the Jews there were the Nazarites, Recha- bites, and Essenes, sects and communities who were vowed to abstinence. One of the five commandments of the Buddhists is directed against drunkenness; and Mahomet, as is well known, forbade wine to all the true believers—a prohibition which the Wahabees hold to be applicable also to tobacco, for the smoking of which they have invented the phrase of "drinking the shameful."

No doubt the teetotal antiquary, whenever he arises, will be able to compile a long list of illustrious abstainers, including saints and martyrs, as well as prelates and soldiers. Amongst them, along with Archbishop Baldwin, Johnson, and eccentrics like Roger Crab, he would have to mention that Andrew Tiraqueau, who was the author of twenty books, and the father of twenty children, and of whom it was written :—

> Here lies a man, who, drinking only water,
> Wrote twenty books, with each had son or daughter ;
> Had he but used the juice of generous vats,
> The world would scarce have held his books and brats.

Towards the end of the last and the early part of the present century the intemperate habits of the people appear to have led to organised efforts to mitigate the evil. The first American Temperance Society is said to have been begun in 1789. Gradually the news of this movement reached the old country, but it does not appear that any organised effort was made until 1829, when a Congregational minister of New Ross, Wexford, Ireland, conceived the idea of transplanting the Temperance Society on Irish soil. The progress made at first was not very remarkable, but after a time associations of this kind arose in various parts of Ireland, Scotland, and England.

By the middle of 1831 some thirty societies were in existence in England, and 100,000 tracts had been put into circulation. The members were pledged to " moderation " in the use of intoxicants, or at most to abstinence

from spirits.   The reformers' zeal did not extend to malt
liquors, which were still considered innocuous.   This was
not, however, sufficient for the more ardent and enthusiastic.
They began to see the difficulty of defining a hard-and-fast
line of moderation.   Indeed, as early as 1817 an abstinence
society had been formed in Skibbereen, in the county of
Cork, and two years later there was at Greenock a Radical
Association whose members had likewise pledged themselves to use no intoxicants.   But it seems as though they
intended this rather as a protest against the high taxation
then levied on many articles.   There was also the Bible
Christian Church in Salford, of which membership was confined to vegetarians and teetotallers.

The modern teetotallers, however, date their origin from
the 1st September, 1832, when, as the result of much
discussion in the existing temperance societies, Mr. Joseph
Livesey and six others signed a pledge "to abstain from all
liquors of an intoxicating quality, whether ale, porter, wine,
or ardent spirits, except as medicine."   Of the "seven men
of Preston," as they have often been called, two broke their
pledge, and of the others two still remain in a green old
age.   These two are Joseph Livesey and John King, who,
together with Mr. Edward Grubb, received silver medals at
the jubilee.   The early teetotallers were animated by a very
earnest missionary spirit, and preached their new doctrine
with great persistence, and with great success.   They travelled
far and near in order to propagate their views, and many
amusing stories are told of the way in which they were
obliged to enlist the interest of their auditors, and of the

devices they found it necessary to employ in order to secure audiences at all.

It was during the Preston race week of 1833 that Livesey, Teare, Anderton, Swindlehurst, Howarth, and Stead started out on the first missionary tour ever undertaken in the interests of teetotalism. They hired a trap, and took with them over 9,000 tracts and a small silk flag bearing a temperance motto. In this fashion they visited Blackburn, Haslingden, Bury, Heywood, Ashton, Oldham, Rochdale, Stockport, Manchester, and Bolton, besides halting at villages on the way. Whilst one waved the flag about, another, the fortunate possessor of a good voice, obtained the use of the bell from the village bellman, and announced in stentorian tones the time and place at which the meeting would be held. It was one of the reformed drunkards of Preston who first applied the word teetotal to express total abstinence from intoxicants. Mr. P. T. Winskill, in his recently issued "History of the Temperance Movement," has entered fully into the origin and meaning of the word. Messrs. Livesey and Teare, he says, agree in ascribing the first application of the word to the principles of total abstinence from intoxicating liquors to Richard Turner, one of the early converts, and a zealous though humble and illiterate advocate. In the month of September, 1833, "Dickey" Turner was speaking at a meeting in the cockpit at Preston, when, in his own peculiar way, he used these words, "I'll have now't to do w' this moderation botheration pledge; I'll be reet down out-and-out tee-tee total for ever and ever." "Well done!" exclaimed the audience. "Well

done, Dickey!" exclaimed Mr. Livesey; "that shall be the
name of our new pledge." Mr. Livesey says it is a mistake
to suppose, as some have done, that the word arose from
the mispronunciation of a stammerer. "The truth is," says
Mr. Livesey, "that Dickey was never at a loss for a word;
if a suitable one was not at his tongue end he coined one."
Dr. F. R. Lees says "that it is a vulgar error to suppose
that he either invented the word or stuttered it forth. The
term," he adds, "has been in common use in Ireland and in
Lancashire these hundred years, and was familiar to the
writer when a lad in that country above forty years ago.
It can be found in the literature of England long prior to
the Preston movement, in application to various things.
Banim, the Irish novelist, employs it. Maginn, in 'Maga,'
uses it; and De Quincey, also a master of English, who
probably acquired it in Lancashire, amidst the idioms .of
which county he spent his early years. Richard Turner
used the word because it had an established meaning. It
was one of those designations to which children and un-
educated persons were apt to give spontaneous expression;
and because it fell in with popular usage and feeling, Mr.
Livesey wisely, or unwisely, adopted it as the name of the
new society. Dickey Turner is buried in St. Peter's Churchyard, Preston, and the inscription on his grave is, 'Beneath
this stone are deposited the remains of Richard Turner,
author of the word teetotal as applied to abstinence from all
intoxicating liquors, who departed this life on the 27th day
of October, 1846, aged 56 years.'" Mr. Charles Hardwick
has informed the writer that he remembers the occasional

use of the word "teetotal" before it was applied to "total abstinence" from intoxicants.

From a statement recently made it would appear that Turner's special use of the word was anticipated. "It appears that in 1819 the Hector Temperance Society was formed in the State of New York on the anti-spirit principle, and that, dissatisfied with this principle as too narrow, some of the members became abstainers from all intoxicants. In 1827 the Lansing Temperance Society was formed, and two pledges were introduced—one against distilled spirits, the other against all alcoholic liquors. The first was marked "O. P." (Old Pledge); the second "T," meaning total. A goodly number signed the latter, and they were spoken of as "T-totalers"—the initial letter "T," and the explanation, "Total," being pronounced as one word. The witness on this point is the Rev. Joel Jewel, of Troy, Bradford county, Pennsylvania, who was the secretary of the Lansing Temperance Society, and is now about eighty years of age." (*Alliance News*, February 17, 1883.)

This apparently only applies to the word as written, not as spoken.

ROBERT WILSON AND THE INVENTION OF
THE STEAM HAMMER.

———o◆o———

An exquisite invention this.

LEIGH HUNT. *Love-letters made of flowers.*

———

THE story of the invention of the steam hammer was
first told by Dr. Samuel Smiles in his "Industrial
Biography," and the narrative has been repeated in the
charming book in which Mr. James Nasmyth has recounted
his autobiography. The idea of a steam hammer certainly
occurred to James Watt, but although he took a patent for
it in 1784 the machine he designed does not appear to have
ever been constructed. Again, in 1806, Mr. William
Deverell obtained protection for a similar mechanical project, but there is no evidence that it ever took practical
shape. In 1837 the Great Britain steamship was in course
of construction, and Mr. Humphries, its engineer, who had
been unable to find a foundry where they would undertake
the forgings required for the paddle-shafts, applied to Mr.
James Nasmyth, then at the head of the Bridgewater

Foundry. The happy thought of a steam hammer occurred to him, and he sent a sketch of it which met with approval, but was not adopted because the screw propeller had proved so decidedly superior to the old system that the enormous engines which Mr. Humphries had designed were set aside. He died of brain fever, " so that neither his great paddle-shaft nor Mr. Nasmyth's steam hammer to forge it was any longer needed." The drawing remained in Mr. Nasmyth's sketch book, but it did not find favour with the English forge masters to whom it was shown. The keen eyes of M. Schneider, of Creusot, however, noticed it on a visit to the Patricroft foundry, over which he was shown by the partner of Mr. Nasmyth, and the latter found it, greatly to his surprise, working at Creusot when he visited that famous establishment in 1840. It is not at all probable that Mr. Nasmyth foresaw the great importance of the new departure he was introducing to the engineering world. He designed the steam hammer to meet a particular case, and it was thought to be applicable only to the largest class of forgings which were not at that time needed with so much frequency as to make it marketable. The utility of the machine was also greatly restricted by the fact that the valve motion was worked only by hand. The special difficulties in the way of providing a self-acting motion apparently proved insuperable to Mr. Nasmyth, for during his absence in 1842 his partner applied to the late Mr. Robert Wilson, who was then manager, and afterwards became the principal of the Bridgewater Foundry. This gentleman, after a few days' consideration of the problem, produced a self-acting motion which gave the steam hammer the importance it now holds as an engineering tool.

The career of Mr. Wilson previous to his connection with the invention of the steam hammer furnishes an interesting example of endeavour and achievement. He was born in 1803 at Dunbar, on the east coast of Scotland, where his father was drowned in the third attempt of the lifeboat to save the remainder of the crew of the frigate Pallas, which was cast ashore in December, 1810. Young Wilson, as a boy, was particularly fond of aquatic amusements of every kind, and as early as 1808 his childish attention was called to a matter with which his name has since become inseparably associated. A soldier who was then stationed at Dunbar fitted out a small fishing boat with a pair of side paddles which proved unsuitable where the surface of the water was at all rough. Wilson as a child was an expert sculler, and the thought occurred to him that if something in the nature of a sculling oar could be fitted to the stern of the vessels it would be free from the objections to side paddles. The problem appears to have interested him greatly, and from time to time recurred to his mind. The sight of an undershot water-wheel, and later of a windmill used at Oxwellmains for threshing corn, brought the matter up again. He learned that it reefed and unreefed its own sails, and turned its face always towards the wind. " How this was effected," he says, " I determined to discover, and a few days after I returned to Oxwellmains, taking with me a small telescope to enable me more closely to examine the mechanical arrangement of the windmill. The mill was not working, and I had, therefore, a better opportunity of studying it. I lay down on the grass field in front of it so as to use my knees as a rest for the telescope, and in this position, while engaged in wonder and admiration, trying to follow and account for the various motions which I knew the mill to have, an idea suddenly occurred to me, which rendered it perfectly clear in what way I could modify the sculling oar so as to make it serve as a means of propelling a vessel." This was in effect by putting it in the form of a wind wheel such as that he had before him. He even tried some unsuccessful experiments with a small model, but the matter dropped until 1821, when the difficulty with which the "Tourist," one of the then new steamers, overcame the ground swell in the barbour of Dunbar led to further experiments with what young Wilson now termed "rough sea or storm paddles." Soon after his father's death Wilson was apprenticed to a joiner, and removed from Dunbar, which, however, he visited in 1821 and 1825, when he again made experiments with his propeller. The necessities of his daily life did not allow Mr. Wilson to give undivided attention to the problem, but it was one which again and again occupied the scanty leisure of his artisan days. In 1827 he made the acquaintance of Mr. James Hunter, who introduced him to the Earl of Lauderdale. That nobleman asked his son, Captain Maitland, to report on an experiment to be made with Wilson's model. The result was satisfactory, and the Earl promised to try to induce the Admiralty to take up the invention. It was shown at the Dunbar Mechanics' Institution, and in 1828 the Highland Society appointed a committee who testified to the success of his plan when tried at Leith in a very heavy sea. The Society granted him £10, but only on condition of receiving his model, which he very reluctantly gave up. His want of means prevented any further action, but in 1832 Mr. Hunter brought the matter before the Scottish Society of Arts, and a committee, which included Sir Thomas Dick Lauder, reported on it. A silver medal was awarded to the inventor, and the Society, through Sir John Sinclair, called the attention of the Admiralty to the subject. The Woolwich officers to whom it was referred made a brief and supercilious report, and the inventor's hopes were dashed to the ground. He was mortified by this rejection, nor was his mortification lessened when he learned that in 1836 Mr. F. P. Smith had patented an "improved propeller" on the screw plan. The Admiralty, after rejecting Wilson and repulsing Ericsson, adopted the patent of Smith, who eventually received a knighthood. One of the officials who, in 1833, reported against the screw propeller of Wilson, in 1840 reported in favour of the screw propeller of Smith. There can be no doubt that serious injustice was done to Mr. Wilson by ignorance or carelessness of the officers of the Admiralty. This may be affirmed without claiming for him any absolute priority in the invention. The French annals record not only the experiments of Sauvage at Boulogne in 1832, but those of Paneton in 1792, of Dubost in 1746, and of Duquet in 1727, whilst quite recently it has been said that the screw propeller was anticipated by the universal genius of Leonardo da Vinci.

These early experiments were not, however, lost. In presenting them Mr. Wilson was developing his inventive faculties, and as recently as 1880 the War Department made a grant of £500 for the use of his double action screw propeller as applied to the fish torpedo.

In 1832 Mr. Wilson was in business as an engineer in Edinburgh, in the North Back of Canongate, but a few years later he migrated to Manchester, and in 1838 was the manager of the famous Bridgewater Foundry at Patricroft, the birthplace of the steam hammer. We have already stated the nature of his connection with the remarkable tool which has been described by Professor Tomlinson as one of "the most perfect of artificial machines, and the noblest triumph of mind over matter that modern English engineers have yet developed." The relative shares in the invention are concisely stated in a letter written by Mr. Holbrook Gaskell, who was the partner of Nasmyth, and was the gentleman who showed the sketch to the appreciative M. Schneider :—"That to Mr. Nasmyth is due the original conception of the direct acting steam hammer I have frequently testified, and am prepared to maintain ; but that either he or any one else had any conception of the great future which awaited his invention I distinctly deny. The hammer was designed, as Mr. Smiles mentions, to provide for a particular exigency. It was thought to be only applicable to the largest class of forgings ; and so rare was the demand at that time for such massive forging that Mr. Nasmyth could not induce any of the proprietors of the great forges of the county to accept the invention on the condition of patenting it for themselves, and ordering a hammer from him.   Seeing that the utility of the machine was extremely restricted by the valve motion being worked only by hand, and, therefore, very slowly, and with much labour, I felt very desirous that it should be made self-acting so that it might be worked at a higher speed, and thereby be adapted to all ranges of forgings from the smallest to the highest.   The result was *your very beautiful invention of the self-acting motion* for which a patent was immediately secured."   There is also an equally explicit statement of the foreman of the smiths, Mr. T. M. Crewdson, who forged " every particle of the first efficient self-acting motion ever made," from the drawings and under the superintendence of Mr. Wilson.   The first hammer was delivered in August, 1843, to the Low Moor Ironworks, and continued in use there until 1853, when Mr. Wilson, who was then engineer of that establishment, added to it what is known as the " circular balanced valve," which he then patented.   In 1856 Mr. James Nasmyth retired from his active industrial career, but has since been often heard of in the still wider world of science.   Mr. Robert Wilson was now recalled from Low Moor, and became the managing partner of the firm of Messrs. Nasmyth, Wilson, and Co.

He maintained the world-wide fame of his firm, and, mindful of his own early difficulties, was ready to smooth the path of those who showed talent and industry.   He died at Matlock, 28th July, and is buried in the pleasant churchyard of St. Catherine's, Barton-on-Irwell.

ELIAS, THE MANCHESTER PROPHET.

Thy voice sounds like a prophet's woe.
FITZ-GREENE HALLECK. *Marco Bozzaris.*

In nature's infinite book of secresy
A little I can read.
SHAKSPERE.

ELLIS HALL was the son of a carpenter in Manchester, and was born in the year 1502. In his early childhood he was noticeable as different from other children, and was teased and persecuted by his brethren on account of the "solitariness, abstinence, and prayer" that marked him even before the age of seven, when he was taken from home to the house that was afterwards that of Gerard, the Attorney-General. Here he was put to the laborious, if not dignified calling of "tournynge of the broche." The scullion boy was not proof against the attacks of love, but having married a wife he looked higher than the kitchen range, and was in a fair way for prosperity as a draper, so that, as he tells us, even when there came a great fall in the value of money, in the reign of Edward VI. his yearly profit amounted to £500.

Whilst giving himself up to the cares of the world, and quite forgetful of his juvenile piety, he had one night what he regarded as a vision, though others might deem it an idle dream. About midnight, as he lay sleepless and pondering over " a great accompte," he heard a voice delivering this message :—" Eli, thou carpenter's son, arise and make thine account quickly ; fast and pray, for the day draweth near." This invocation was thrice repeated, and then there was a great light, after which he saw the figure of a man in white, with five bleeding wounds. This figure vanished in the heavens that opened to receive him. This vision did not deter Ellis from the prosecution of his calling, but soon he was prostrated by disease, and as he lay bedfast the vision came again, and told him that he was " elect and chosen of God to declare and pronounce unto his people His word." Ellis objected that he was unlearned, but the vision commanded him to " Write of the revelation that thou hast seen of baptism, repentance and amendment of life, and show it to the magistrates and rulers, and that which thou shalt write shall be put into thy head by the Holy Ghost." Then Ellis was taken first to heaven, and afterwards to hell. The torments that awaited him if he did not amend were shown him, and also the place reserved for him in heaven if he followed God's will were shown to him. He claimed that this journey into the supernatural world was not in the spirit, but in the flesh, and that for two nights and one day he was absent, and not seen of any man. This was from the 9th to the 11th of April, 1552. He was commanded to watch and pray for seven years, and to write for three years and a half. In this space of time he wrote a small book of "Obedience," and one without a title, known as the "Great Book." After he began the work of composition he ceased to eat fish or flesh, and gave over the use of wine. He claimed to have written the book on his knees.

Ellis Hall went to London in 1562, and in his dress of camel's hair attracted great attention. He called himself "Ely, the Carpenter's Son," and declared that he was the messenger of God, speaking and working by heavenly inspiration. He made his way to Gravesend, and endeavoured to make his way into the Queen's presence chamber. Bishop Pilkington — another Lancashire man — preached before the Queen in exposure of the claims of the Manchester prophet, who was examined before the Bishop of London on the 12th of June, 1562. Then he was brought before the Earl of Bedford; Lord Clinton, the Lord High Admiral of England; Lord Cobham, the Warden of the Cinque Ports; Sir A. Cave, the Chancellor of the Duchy of Lancaster; and Sir Richard Sackfield, the "Treasurer" of the Queen's Exchequer. The examination was at the Savoy, on the 17th of June, 1562. He gave a straightforward account of his life and visions, and ended thus :—"Since wch tyme I have apparrelled my selfe thus as ye see, and goe wolward to thintent to bringe the fleshe in subjeceon to the sowle; neyther have I eten at any tyme this yeare and this halfe any fleshe, but white meat and to the same yntent, and ever senc that tyme have geven myselfe to my former vertuous lyvinge in fasting and prayinge, and ever since that tyme have wrytten and by God's devyne powre coulde wryte although but small as I protest before yor honors all that before that tyme I could not wryte. Thus have I ever since settled myselfe to wryte God's holye wyll and contaimdements (sic), and dystrybuted my goods emongs my kynsmen and pore people makinge proclemacon that yf any mann coulde com unto whome I ought any thinge unto for every pennye I wolde make him double amends. Also that sythens that tyme I have wrytten this booke which I have here brought before yow entendinge (God wyllinge) to delyver the same vnto my prynce before that any anye mann do throughly peruse yt. Neyther have I attayned to this end by any worldlye means. Thus besechinge yer honors all that yf theise my sayings can be provyd false in any pointe, lett me suffer deathe to ensample of all others."

There was but little of the law's delay in dealing with heretics, for, on the 26th June he was placed in the pillory in Cheape with this inscription written on a paper over his head, "ffor seducinge the people by publyshyng ffalce Revelaceons."

The unfortunate visionary was then taken back to prison, and the last glimpse we have of him is the memoranda made by Stowe :—

Anno, 1563, the 27th day of July, beynge Tuesday, Elys Hawll, of Manchester, was whipt at Bedlem by to mynysters or prechars, Philpot, a parson of Sent Myhells in Cornhyll, and Yownge, b parson of Sent Bartylmews ye Lytyll, Fulclres ye comon cryar of London stondyne by.

In Anno 1564 (accoumptynge ye yere to begyn ye xxv. of

Marche), the xxv. day of February, at xj. of ye cloke in ye nyghte, deseasyd the abovesayd Elisens Hawll, and was buryed on Shordche Churcheyarde on ye Twesday, and ye xxvij. day of February, at xj. of ye cloke before none.

A curious circumstance about the punishment of the Manchester Prophet is, that he was flogged by two ministers.

The data as to Ellis Hall is to be found in Strype's "Annals of the Reformation," vol. 1. p. 469 ; Earwaker's "Local Gleanings," vol. 1, p. 72, 84 ; "Three Fifteenth Century Chronicles, with Historical Memoranda," by John Stowe (Camden Society, 1880). The MS. "Visions of Eliseus Hall," in metre, was in the library of John Parker, son of Archbishop Parker.

WESTHOUGHTON FACTORY FIRE.

Famine is on thy cheeks,
Need and oppression starveth in thy eyes,
Contempt and beggary hang upon thy back,
The world is not thy friend, nor the world's law.

SHAKSPERE.

THE year 1812 was one of great suffering for the working classes of Lancashire. The manufacturing districts were hotbeds of disaffection, and there is too much reason to think that the Government, instead of redressing grievances, encouraged a system of espionage by which the unwary were seduced into overt acts of sedition, and then heavily punished. The simple-minded and suffering people were taught by the spies to lay all their sufferings at the door of authority, and when their victims had been betrayed into treason the informers reaped a bloody harvest.

The handloom weavers were exasperated at the introduction of steam power into the mills, which they expected would still further reduce their earnings. There were riots at Manchester, Middleton, and various other places. In some places the mob contented themselves with sacking provision shops, in others they burned mills and destroyed machinery. The burning of Westhoughton factory was one of the most lamentable of these deplorable incidents.

The heavy war taxes, the depression of trade, and the high price of provisons had brought the weavers to the verge of starvation. Wheat ranged £6 to £7 per quarter, and sometimes families went for whole days without food. The narrative of one of the ringleaders in the Westhoughton affair, who had escaped conviction, has been printed. Of course his name is not given. About November, 1811, he says, midnight meetings began to be held in the neighbour-hood of Chowbent (Atherton), and a brotherhood was formed, bound by oath, with the object of "revolutionising the country." At one of these secret assemblies, held at Clapperfold, March 20, 1812, a man named Sidlow made a violent speech, concluding with a proposal to burn Westhoughton Factory. This was agreed to, and the 19th of April was appointed for the execution of this dreadful project. There were in the throng, however, many "black-faces" as the spies were called, and the magistrates appear to have been fully cognisant of what was going on. The factory was guarded night and day by armed men. On the 19th of April there was a gathering on Dean Moor, at which the "blackfaces" are said to have formed a fourth of the assembly. The military were in waiting to "cut up" the assailants. Incited by the spies the weavers set out, and on the road they met a man named Holland Bowden, and in accordance with a resolution to twist or puff *(swear* or *shoot)* every one they met he was forced to take their seditious oath. On their march something suspicious was observed, and the enterprise was abandoned for that night. On the 24th it was, however, carried into effect. They formed in the Market Place, and marched four deep to the factory, which was heavily barricaded. Although the door was cut "almost to matches" they could not force an entrance, and a man was put through a window to remove the fastenings. The cloth was wrapped round the beams, the wooden looms were quickly smashed, and the mill, a few moments earlier a model of cleanliness and neatness, was strewn with the fragments " like swathes of grass." John Seddon then said, "The egg is broken, let us burn the shell." A shovel of fire was placed in a calico " cut," laid down on the floor, and the broken looms piled around it. A hogshead of tallow was rolled into the fire. A number of women danced a reel around the blazing heap. Then the cry was raised, " Every man to his tents, O Israel," and each one tried to get home unobserved.

The magistrates appeared on the scene and read the Riot Act, and the Scots Greys were marched to the scene of the disturbance. A number of arrests were made, and the men sent to Lancaster. The rioters, who were placed on their trial, were Adam Bullough, whose age is not given; John Brownlow, 15 ; William Kay, 33 ; Abraham Charlson, 16 ; Bold Howarth, 32 ; Job Fletcher, 34 ; John Shuttleworth, 59 ; Samuel Radcliffe, 35 ; Robert Woodward, 27 ; Thomas Kerfoot, 26 ; John Charlson, 34 ; James Smith, 31 ; Mary Cannon, 19 ; and Lydia Molyneux, 15. The men charged with administering the oath to

Holland Bowden were Christopher Medcalf, 41 ; James Brierley, 30 ; Henry Thwaite, 24 ; Joseph Clement, 21 ; William Gifford or Clifford, 40 ; Thomas Pickup, 51 ; John Heys, 37 ; John Hurst, 37 ; Peter Topping, 35 ; Joseph Greenhalgh, 22 ; and Samuel Radliffe, 35. Hurst, it is said, went by the name of " General Ludd." This name of terror was doubtless used by various individuals in the different districts that were then in a disturbed condition.

Special assizes were opened at Lancaster on the 25th May before Baron Thomson and Sir Simon Le Blanc. The commission was opened on Saturday, and on the Tuesday following, at eight o'clock in the morning, the rioters were charged with setting fire to (or aiding and assisting therein) the weaving mill, warehouse, and loom shop of Thomas Rowe and Thomas Duncough. The trial lasted until eight at night, when Abraham Charlson, Fletcher, Kerfoot, and Smith were found guilty, and the rest acquitted. Those who were found guilty of administering the unlawful oath were Medcalf, Brierley, Thwaite, Pickup, Hurst, and Radcliffe, and they were sentenced to transportation. Charlson, Fletcher, Kerfoot, and Smith were sentenced to death.

The trial of the Westhoughton rioters was followed by those of the men from Middleton and Manchester, and whilst these were proceeding the Westhoughton men were speculating as to their sentences. " I believe," says the rioter already quoted, " it never entered the mind of any of them that they should get more than three or six months' imprisonment. They were called upon to receive their sentences, and I shall never forget the look of horror on the

face of Job Fletcher.   I was getting some dinner ready for
him when he went, and he came back in a few minutes;
grasped me by the collar in a frenzied manner.   ' O dear,
dear,' cried he, ' I must be hanged.'   Others came in who
received the same sentence, and the most heart-rending
scene took place that it is possible for the mind to conceive.
Some threw themselves on the floor, others tore their hair
from their heads, bitterly cursing the witnesses who had
appeared against them, and lamenting that they must never
more see their families.   They were taken from us to the
condemned cells, and I never saw any of them more."   The
fate of these unfortunate persons is briefly stated in the
Gentleman's Magazine: — " June 13.   Eight rioters, who
were convicted at the Special Assizes at Lancaster, viz.,
J. Smith, T. Kerfoot, J. Fletcher, A. Charlson, J. Howarth,
J. Lee, T. Hoyle, and Hannah Smith (for stealing potatoes)
underwent their sentence.   While in confinement they
manifested the greatest indifference and unconcern, but
were at length brought to a sense of their condition, and died
penitent."   Hannah Smith was a woman of 54, one of a
riotous crowd who stole some potatoes at Bank Top, Manchester.   Howarth, Lee, and Hoyle had, during a riot,
broken into a shop in Deansgate, stolen bread, cheese,
and potatoes.

According to the tradition of the neighbourhood the boy
Charlson was a cripple, and was hoisted on a man's shoulders
in order to break a window with his crutch.   He is described
as 16 in the reports of the assize, but it has been, said that
he was in reality only 12 years old.   The poor lad, when in

the hands of the hangman, cried out, "Oh, mammy, mammy!"

The riot had the effect of calling attention to the want and starvation that was existing, and in the *Manchester Mercury* of June 16 we learn that "On Saturday week 360 families of the poor inhabitants of Westhoughton were relieved with oatmeal gratis by a subscription in the said township."

We have spoken of the spies. One of these, who had achieved infamy in 1801, is said to have had his services overlooked by his employers, and to have been one of those hung at Lancaster in 1812. The spy system was eloquently exposed by Dr. Robert Eveleigh Taylor in his letter on the Lancashire Riots of 1812. There are also references to the subject in Prentice's "Historical Sketches," and Brimelow's "Political History of Bolton." The story of the riot has also been told in a rhyming chronicle:—"A Tragedy: the Burning of Westhoughton Cotton Mill in 1812." A poem by John Clough (Bolton, *Journal* Office, 1882). This includes some lines about the "Snydale Ghost," which, as containing a bit of local folk-lore may be quoted as a relief to the ghastly narrative of the Westhoughton riots.

> At midnight hour, when all was still,
> This ghost would wander o'er the hill;
> The object of its nightly round
> Was thought some treasure in the ground.
> With bated breath, and blanched face,
> The traveller o'er this lonely place
> Would fancy in each clump of trees
> The weird and uncouth form he sees

Of Worthington, whose wandering lo
Was nightly round this haunted spot.
The ghost 'tis said was laid at Deane,
To come no more whilst holly is green,
Or water down a ditch should run,
Save once in years of twenty-one.
They used to say this was its hire,
Till once it came, the barn took fire,
And Snydale barn with all its store
Burnt to the ground to rise no more.
But Snydale Hall may still be seen
Where waters run, and holly is green.
With a young pullet, it is said,
The ghost of Worthington was laid ;
Whilst others in these later days
Say it was frightened by the Greys,
Whose clattering marching on the road
Drove it to seek its last abode.

GEORGE FOX'S FIRST ENTRY
INTO LANCASHIRE.

And they that turn many to righteousness shall shine as the stars for ever and ever.

DANIEL xii. 3.

WE who see the members of the Society of Friends, staid and almost universally respectable and respected, can have little real conception of the time when they were hemmed in by a ring of cruel persecution, and themselves ablaze with fiery enthusiasm. George Fox, the founder of the Quakers, came of godly lineage. His father was called, by his neighbours, "Righteous Christer," and his mother "was of the stock of the martyrs." He was born in 1624, at Drayton-in-the-Clay, in Leicestershire, and in his childhood was remarkable for his quaint unchildish ways, not delighting in innocent play, but rather noted for a gravity beyond his years. When nineteen, he says, "At the command of God, on the 9th of the 7th month, 1643, I left my relations, and broke off all familiarity or fellowship with old or young." He talked with many professors of religion, but obtained no help from them. On returning to his own people some advised him to marry, others to turn soldier. An " ancient priest," to whom he unfolded the troubles which now agitated his soul, prescribed, as a cure, tobacco and psalm singing ! Neither remedy suited George Fox. He now began to hold that doctrine of the inner light which is the basis of all mystical philosophy. By inspiration and vision he held that he had attained the truth he had so long sought after. " I heard," he says, " of a woman in Lancashire, that had fasted two and twenty days, and I travelled to see her ; but when I came to her I found she was under a temptation. When I had spoken to her what I had from the Lord I left her, her father being one high in profession. Passing on I went among the professors at Duckingfield and Manchester, where I stayed awhile, and declared truth among them." This was the beginning of the ministry of George Fox in the year 1648. Local tradition points out the stone cross, at Dukinfield, as the place where his public ministry commenced. The cross no longer holds its original position. The base was in the possession of the late Mr. Alfred Aspland, F.R.C.S.

He now began to move about the country preaching his new doctrine, reproving sinners, and exhorting rich and poor to the due performance of their duty. His religion was of a very practical kind, and he laid small stress upon accuracy of belief that did not involve rightness of life. He was the very incarnation of plain speaking, and went right to the heart of things. To take the hat off in honour of a fellow-creature seemed to him a species of idolatry. So he refused to render "hat-honour" to anyone, and addressed "thee" and "thou" alike to high and low. He refused to take oaths of any kind. He refused to bear arms or pay tithes. This plain, honest, sober-living countryman, who had no awe of dignities before him, was to be a trouble and a stumbling block to the authorities. There was no common ground between them. He held the witness of the Spirit to be higher than the ruling of the law or the letter of the Scripture. Authority he set at nought, for he felt that he had the certain word of the Lord to deliver to his fellow men. So he went into courts of law and exhorted judges to act justly, he bade publicans not to make men drunk, he declaimed against May games and feasts, he stood in the Market Place and denounced the frauds of the hucksters, he cried out against mountebanks and music, he exhorted schoolmasters and heads of families to bring up the children committed to them in the fear of the Lord. But that which chiefly excited his indignation was what he calls the black earthy spirit of the priests. The church bell had no sweet sound for his ears, but "was just like a market bell to gather people together, that the priest might expose his wares to sale." He was imprisoned at Nottingham "as a youth" who had disturbed the congregation by denying the truth of the doctrine in the parson's sermon.

In 1652 occurred a memorable visit to Lancashire. George Fox, coming into the county from Yorkshire, felt "moved by the Lord" to ascend the "very great and high hill" of Pendle. From its lofty summit he saw not only the sea bordering upon the country, but the places where there was to be a great gathering of the people to his faith. "As I went down I found a spring of water in the side of the hill, with which I refreshed myself, having eaten or drunk but little in several days before." After journeying in West-moreland he came to Newton-in-Cartmell, where the clergy-man did not relish his unasked-for assistance in preaching at the chapel. In consequence, a rude multitude seized Fox— guilty of the reformer's usual crime of zeal out of season— who hailed him from the church, and finally thew him head-long over a stone wall. In this turmoil Fox spoke to one who was taking notes of the clergyman's discourse. This was John Braithwaite. Soon after we find him at the house of Judge Fell, at Swarthmoor, disputing with a neighbour-ing clergyman. Margaret Fell became a follower, and her husband, though not one of the Friends, always treated them tenderly. How greatly they laid themselves open to the cruelty of their adversaries may be seen from George Fox's narrative of an incident which occurred in 1652. "After this," he says, "on a lecture day I was moved to go to the steeplehouse at Ulverstone, where there were abundance of professors, priests, and people. I went up near to Priest Lampitt, who was blustering on in his preaching; and after the Lord had opened my mouth to speak, John Sawrey, the justice, came to me and said, 'if I would speak according to the Scripture I should speak.' I admired at him for speak-ing so to me, for I did speak according to the Scriptures, and bring the Scriptures to prove what I had to say; for I had something to speak to Lampitt and to them. Then he said that I should not speak, contradicting himself. . . .

The people were quiet and heard me gladly, until this Justice Sawrey, who was the first stirrer-up of cruel persecution in the north, incensed them against me, and set them on to hate, beat, and bruise me. Then, on a sudden, the people were in a rage, and fell upon me in the steeple-house before his face ; they knocked me down, kicked me, trampled upon me ; and so great was the uproar, that some people tumbled over their seats for fear. At last he came and took me from the people, led me out of the steeple-house, and put me into the hands of the constables and other officers, bidding them whip me out of the town. They led me about a quarter of a mile, some taking hold by my collar, and some by my arms and shoulders, and shook and dragged me along. Many friendly people being come to the market, and some of them to the steeple-house to hear me, divers of these they knocked down also, and broke their heads, so that the blood ran down from several of them ; and Judge Fell's son running after, to see what they would do with me, they threw him into a ditch of water, some of them crying, 'knock the teeth out of his head.' Now when they haled me to the common moss-side, a multitude of people following, the constables and other officers gave me some blows over my back with their willow-rods, and so thrust me among the rude multitude, who, having furnished themselves, some with staves, some with hedge-stakes, and others with holm or holly-bushes, fell upon me, and beat me on my head, arms, and shoulders, till they had deprived me of sense, so that I fell down on the wet common. When I recovered again, and saw myself lying in a watery common, and the people

about me, I lay still a little while; and the power of the
Lord sprang through me, and the eternal refreshings
refreshed me, so that I stood up again in the strengthening
power of the Eternal God; and, stretching out my arms
amongst them, I said, with a loud voice, 'Strike again; here
are my arms, my head, and my cheeks.' There was in the
company a mason, a professor, but a rude fellow; he, with
his walking rule-staff, gave me a blow with all his might, just
over the back of my hand, as it was stretched out; with
which blow my hand was so bruised, and my arm so be-
numbed, that I could not draw it unto me again; so that
some of the people cried out, 'he hath spoiled his hand for
ever having the use of it any more.' But I looked at it in
the love of God (for I was in the love of God to them all
that had persecuted me), and after a while the Lord's power
sprang through me again, and through my hand and arm, so
that in a moment I recovered strength in my hand and arm in
the sight of them all. Then they began to fall out among
themselves, and some of them came to me and said if I
would give them money they would secure me from the rest.
But I was moved of the Lord to declare to them the word
of life, and showed them their false Christianity, and the
fruits of their priest's ministry; telling them they were more
like heathens and Jews than true Christians. Then was I
moved of the Lord to come up again through the midst of
the people, and go into Ulverstone market. As I went, there
met me a soldier with his sword by his side; 'Sir,' said he
to me, 'I see you are a man, and I am ashamed and grieved
that you should be thus abused;' and he offered to assist me

in what he could. But I told him the Lord's power was over all ; so I walked through the people in the market, and none of them had power to touch me then. But some of the market people abusing some Friends in the market, I turned me about and saw this soldier among them with his naked rapier, whereupon I ran in amongst them, and catching hold of his hand that his rapier was in, I bid him put up his sword again, if he would go along with me ; for I was willing to draw him out from the company, lest some mischief should be done. A few days after seven men fell upon this soldier and beat him cruelly, because he had taken part with Friends and me ; for it was the manner of the persecutors of that country for twenty or forty people to run upon one man. And they fell so upon Friends in many places, that they could hardly pass the highways—stoning, beating, and breaking their heads. When I came to Swarthmore, I found the Friends there dressing the heads and hands of Friends and friendly people, which had been broken or hurt that day by the professors and hearers of Lampitt, the priest. My body and arms were yellow, black, and blue, with the blows and bruises I received amongst them that day. Now began the priests to prophesy again, that within half a year we should be all put down and gone." He was afterwards imprisoned in Lancaster Castle.

Such was George Fox's early reception in Lancashire, and yet he reaped a great harvest in the county that used him so cruelly at first.

THE LIVERPOOL TRAGEDY.

Murder most foul, as in the best it is ;
But this most foul, strange, and unnatural.

SHAKSPERE.

A MONGST the street ballads of the present century is one, entirely destitute of literary merit, entitled " The Liverpool Tragedy," which narrates the murder of a traveller slain for the sake of his money by a wretched couple, who afterwards find that the victim was their son, who had returned home to share with them his hard earned wealth.

The *Neue Freie Presse* of Vienna, early in June, 1880, gave currency to the following narrative of crime :— " Fifteen years ago a young Viennese parted from his mother and two brothers to seek his fortune in America. No news ever came of him ; he was supposed to be dead, and lamented as such. Last month, however, the two brothers received the visit of a stranger, who was no other than the supposed defunct. The delight of the recognition may be imagined, and we may be sure that it was not diminished when the wanderer spread out on the table before his brothers' eyes the 300,000 florins which he had brought back with him from America. They would not, however, keep their recovered brother to themselves, and told him that their mother kept an inn in a neighbouring village. It was agreed that the long-lost son should not at once reveal himself to his mother, but should first go to the place *incognito*, and that then, after he had spent two days under his mother's roof, his brothers should rejoin him there to witness his revelation of himself to his mother, and celebrate the reunion of the family by an impromptu festival. But the fifteen years of absence had so changed the son that his mother did not recognise him, and when, before going to his room for the night, the young man begged his hostess to take charge of his 300,000 florins for him, she had no idea who it was that reposed in her such extraordinary trust. Never in her life had she seen such a mass of gold; she could not sleep for the demon of cupidity gnawing at her heart, and yielding at last to the temptation, she took a razor, crept up to the traveller's room, and severed his carotid artery with a single stroke. The body she concealed in a corner of the cellar. Two days afterwards the brothers arrived, and asked if a strange traveller had not come to the inn. The mother grew horribly pale, and, pressed by questions, ended by a full confession. When told who had been her victim, she ran to deliver herself to justice, crying out in the midst of her sobs, 'Kill me, miserable that I am ; I have murdered my son!'"

It will strike those who are familiar with a once famous, but now almost forgotten, play, that this narrative, as well as the story of "The Liverpool Tragedy," contains the exact plot of George Lillo's "Fatal Curiosity."

Lillo's piece was first performed at the Little Theatre in the Haymarket in 1736, and in the following year it was printed as "a true tragedy of three acts." It was frequently acted, and in 1782 George Colman brought out an adaptation of it. In 1784 another adaptation was produced at Covent Garden. It was from the pen of Henry Mackenzie who prefixed the title of "The Shipwreck" to that given by Lillo. The play was the subject of high praise by James Harris, who, in his "Philosophical Inquiries," says, that in this tragedy we find the model of a perfect fable.

It was, perhaps, the eulogy of Harris that led both Colman and Mackenzie to avail themselves of the beauties of the piece whilst endeavouring to remove its blemishes. Lillo, it will be seen, calls it a true tragedy. In fact his play was founded upon a pamphlet called, "Newes from Perin in Cornwall, of a most bloody and unexampled Murther, very lately committed by a Father on his owne Sonne (who was lately returned from the Indyes), at the instigation of a merciless Stepmother, Together with their several most wretched Endes; being all performed in the Month of September last, Anno 1618.," 4to. B. L.

The only copy known of this tract is in the Bodleian Library. The event is recorded also in William Sanderson's "Compleat History of the Lives and Reigns of Mary, Queen of Scotland, and of her Son James" (London, 1656), and in Thomas Frankland's "Annals of James I. and Charles I."

(London, 1681). Baker, in his "Biographia Dramatica," has quoted the last named authority.

Dunlop mentions the same story as told by Vincenzo Rota in one of the late *novelle*, written early in the last century, but not printed until 1794. Here the murder is located at Brescia. Dunlop mentions another version, where the tragedy is said to have happened at a Norman inn. He also states that Werner's "Twenty-fourth of February" is founded on a similar incident.

Lillo's play has been both printed in Germany, and translated into German in the last century. These circumstances seem to warrant us in supposing that the Viennese horror is due to the ingenuity of some purveyor of news, who, for motives best known to himself, but still not difficult to guess at, has passed off an old tragedy as police news.

How accurately he had gauged the public taste may be judged from the fact that his story was copied in a great number of newspapers in Europe and America. London, Philadelphia, Manchester, and Constantinople were alike interested.

But had the pamphlet on which Lillo bases his plot any foundation in fact? The Cornish historians are not, indeed, silent upon the subject; but all rest their case upon the pamphlet, which has all the air of one of those imaginative news letters in which the writer draws upon his fancy for his facts. If this surmise be correct it must be admitted that in this case his imagination has served him well.

LANCASHIRE PROVERBS.

Proverbs are the texts of common life.

L. C. GENT. *Dictionary of English Proverbs.*

THE excellence of the collection of "English Proverbs and Proverbial Phrases," edited by Mr. W. Carew Hazlitt, has been so generally recognised that the new edition, which is "greatly enlarged and carefully revised" (published by Messrs. Reeves and Turner in 1882), will be warmly welcomed by those who delight in those quaint sayings which are said to preserve the wisdom of many and the wit of one. In addition to what are usually known as proverbs —things easy to recognise though difficult to define—Mr. Hazlitt includes in his widespread net many local phrases which, from their traditional currency, may be reckoned as part of the unwritten culture of the commonalty. Several of these relate to Lancashire, and were supplied to Mr. Hazlitt by the spontaneous courtesy of the late Mr. John Higson, to Lees, a ripe antiquary, whose death was a great loss to local archæology. The greater part of these sayings refer to specific places in County Palatine. Some are mere rhymes

for the better recollection of certain facts or fictions in connection with scenery or natural phenomena. Thus :—

> Irk, Irwell, Medlock, and Tame,
> When they meet with the Mersey do lose their name.

These are names of small streams, which, by joining the
larger river, lose their separate existence. Similar is the
well-known Mytton rhyme :—

> The Hodder, the Calder, the Ribble, and Rain,
> All meet in a point on Mytton's domain.

Another version runs :—

> Hodder and Calder and Ribble and Rain,
> All meet together in Mytton demesne.

A third is of a depreciatory character :—

> The Hodder, the Calder, Ribble and Rain,
> All joined together can't carry a bean.

" As old as Pendle Hill " is a Lancashire method of expressing the superlative of antiquity, and truly this one of the
brotherhood of the "everlasting hills" may well be the
symbol of a hoary past. The native is not altogether indis-
posed to slightly exaggerate its greatness :—

> Pendle, Ingleborough, and Penigent,
> Are the three highest hills between Scotland and Trent.

Another version runs :—

> Pendle, Penigent and Ingleborough,
> Are the three highest hills all England thorough.

"These three hills," says John Ray, "are in sight of each other ; Pendle, on the edge of Lancashire ; Penigent and Ingleborough, near Settle, in Yorkshire, and not far from Westmoreland. In Wales, I think Snowdon, Cader Idris, and Plinlimmon are higher." Mr. Hazlitt adds :—"Grey Friar, in the north of Lancashire, and Whernside, in York-shire, are loftier than Pendle Hill. But in such cases as this, the country folks are sure to maintain the honour of their own, in spite of facts and ordnance surveys."

> When Pendle wears its woolly cap,
> The farmers all may take a nap.

There is a similar saying as to Old Know, near Rochdale. Another great Lancashire Hill is Rivington Pike, which rises 1,545 feet above the sea level. The weather prophets have not neglected this indicator, and affirm that—

> If Rivington Pike do wear a hood,
> Be sure the day will ne'er hold good.

Another proverb has given rise to some misconception :—

> Kent and Keer
> Have parted many a good man and his meer.

This is given by Mr. Higson, who observes that these two rivers in Lancashire are "fatal or dangerous to persons attempting to ford them with their horses or mares." Pro-fessor Skeat includes this in his edition of Pegge's Kent-icisms, and explains "Keer" to mean (probably) "care." "The river Kent, at low water, flows in several channels over the sands to the middle of Morecambe Bay. The

Keer enters upon the sands in a broad and rapid current, rendering the passage over it at times more dangerous than fording the Kent. Many have perished in fording both rivers when swollen, and in crossing the adjacent sands without due regard to the state of the tide." Such is the explanation given in "Lancashire Legends" by Harland and Wilkinson.

Lancashire is famous for its mosses, but only that of Pilling appears to have attained proverbial renown. "Never done, like Pilling Moss," is by no means a bad way of expressing a lengthy continuity. Speculation as to the origin of these great sealike wastes must often have entered the mind of the curious beholder. The favourite solution of the enigma would seem to be :—

> Once a wood, then a sea,
> Now a moss, and e'er will be.

There is another saying : "God's grace and Pilling Moss are boundless." Many of these rhymes are satirical allusions to various places and their people :—

> Preston for panmugs,
> Huyton for pride,
> Childwall for toiling,
> And playing beside.

Another version runs :—

> Prescot, Huyton, and merry Childow,
> Three parish churches all in a row :
> Prescot for mugs, Huyton for ploydes,
> Childow for ringing and singing besides.

"Ployde" is a word that has escaped our local glossary-makers. It is interpreted as "merry meetings," although some think that ploughs are meant.

There are various rhymes about Preston, of which the best known is :—

> Proud Preston,
> Poor people ;
> High church,
> Low steeple.

Mr. Higson gives a version of the same proverb applied to another town :—

> Proud Ashton, poor people,
> Ten bells, and an old crackt steeple.

Mr. Higson remarks: "This must have originated many years ago, as the church was damaged by a thunderstorm in January, 1791, and the tower rebuilt in 1820-1. No one but an Ashtonian born and bred can pronounce the name of their town as they do. It is between Ash'on and Esh'n."

"Like Colne clock, always at one," is a way of saying that a person or thing is always the same. Another proverb given on the authority of Mr. Higson has a very modern smack and was probably applied to the local scene by an admirer of Sir Walter Scott :—

> He who would see old Hoghton right,
> Must view it by the pale moonlight.

Here is a local challenge which has probably been the prelude to many a well-fought field :—

Th' Abbey Hey bull-dogs drest i' rags,
Dar' no' com' out to th' Gorton lads.

Miss E. S. Holt has recorded this enigmatical rhyme :—

Abraham, Isaac, and Jacob
Lived in a little house a·bit aboon Bacup ;
Abr'am delved and Isaac span,
And Jacob ran about with a little kitty-can.

(Old South-East Lancashire, p. 49.)

The good qualities of certain foods is set forth in the following cautious rhyme :—

In Oldham brewis, wet and warm,
And Rochdale puddings there's no harm.

" Brewis," it may be necessary to explain, even to some Lancashire readers, is oatcake, or bread toasted and soaked in broth or stew. The word is of Welsh origin.

There is a curious saying that—

In Rochdale,
Strangers prosper, natives fail.

Which we may hope is accurate to the extent of one half. The following is somewhat enigmatical :—" The constable of Oppenshaw sets beggars in stocks at Manchester." This, say Harland and Wilkinson, " may mean that when the constable of Openshaw found Manchester sparks enjoying themselves too freely in his district he could follow them home, and then have them placed in the stocks."

A local way of expressing the famous land of Weiss-nichtwo is to say that it is " Neither in Cheshire nor Chowbent." Mr. Hazlitt will, perhaps, allow us to protest against the misprint of "Chawbent." Some of the phrases are mere meaningless nicknames. Thus, Mr. Hazlitt gives "Oldham rough heads, Boughton trotters, Smo'field cossacks, Heywood monkey town." In this, Boughton stands for Bolton. Many others, like "Bury muffs," "Smo-bridge sondknockers," "Middleton moonrakers," &c., might be added to the uncomplimentary list. Perhaps the best known of these is that which draws a nice distinction between "Liverpool gentlemen and Manchester men." "This saying," says Mr. Hazlitt, "which is, of course, a sneer at the inferior breeding of the Mancunians, may be thought to be out of date now, since assuredly there is as much culture at least in Manchester as at Liverpool." Another saying aimed at the Mancunians is :—

> Manchester bred :
> Long in the arms,
> And short in the head.

The Manchester men may, however, console their offended dignity by reflecting that the same sneer has been addressed to the men of Cheshire and Derbyshire. One of the poets of the hill county has indignantly retorted :—

> I' Darbyshire who're born and bred,
> Are strong i' th' arm, but weak i' th' head :
>   So th' lying proverb says.
> Strength i' th' arm, who doubts shall feel ;
> Strength i' th' head, its power can seal
>   The lips that scoff always.

> The jealous jade, nor Derby born
> Where praise wor due pour'd forth bu' scorn
>   An' lying words let faw.
> But far above the proverb stands,
> The Truth, that God's almighty hands
> Ha' welded strength an' mind in one,
> And poured it down i' plenty on
>   Born Darbyshire men aw.

Another "rhyme" throws some doubt on the architectural orthodoxy of the Wigan church builders. "Maudlin maudlin, we began, and built t' church steeple t' wrang side on." "The steeple," says Mr. Higson, "is built on the north side, at the junction of nave and chancel." The vanished glories of Ribchester are set forth in the boast :—

> It is written upon a wall in Rome,
> Ribchester was as rich as any town in Christendom.

"As throng as Knott Mill Fair" and "As thrunk as Eccles wakes" need no explanation.

The rhymes as to the Black Knight of Ashton have been noticed elsewhere in this volume.

Amongst the many prophetical sayings once current in many parts is the following :—

> When all England is aloft,
> Weel are they that are in Christ's Croft ;
> And where should Christ's Croft be,
> But between Ribble and Mersey ?

This is given by Hollingworth, who, writing in the seventeenth century, identifies the croft as the name given to the lands granted by the Conqueror to Roger de Poictou, " inter Ripa et Mersham." Another version is :—

> When all the world shall be aloft,
> Then Hallamshire shall be God's Croft.

This " ould prophesy," as Hollingworth calls it, reappears in the vaticinations of the lugubrious Nixon :—" One asked Nixon where he might be safe in those days?" He answered, " In God's Croft, between rivers Mersey and Dee." The meaning of " Beyond Lawrence of Lancashire " is not very apparent, but the phrase itself is an old one. " He has Lathom and Knowsley," is a Lancashire phrase intended to convey an idea of the superlative in personal possessions. The Bab Balladist of these modern days avers that no Saxon can pretend to an " affection for pipes," but it would appear that our ancestors thought otherwise, and both Lincolnshire and Lancashire were celebrated for their bagpipes. " Like a Lancashire bagpipe " is quoted by Mr. Hazlitt from a tract of the 17th century, and in the reign of James I. the name of Thomas Basset, "the Lancashire bagpipe," occurs in the order of a Masque. " He's in a St. Giles's sweat," or, in the vernacular, " He's in a Sent Gheil's swat," although given as current in the county, is not one in which Lancashire men can have any special property, nor is it one that they would desire to claim, for the meaning is—" He lies in bed while his clothes are being mended." St. Giles is adopted by beggars as their patron saint.

The love of good cheer is witnessed by the old saying :—

> He that would take a Lancashire man at any time or tide,
> Must bait his hook with a good egg pie, or an apple with a red side.

"This," says Mr. Hazlitt, "is given with a slight variation in 'Wit and Drollery,' 1661, p. 250, 'He that will fish for,' &c., and it is also in the edition of the same work printed in 1682. It occurs in what is called 'The Lancashire Song,' apparently a mere string of whimsical scraps."

There is an oft quoted saying,

> Lancashire law,
> No stakes, no draw.

A proverb that has often saved a luckless gamester from the payment of his "debts of honour." Another saying about the county that has been curiously verified on several occasions in recent years is—"What Lancashire thinks to-day, England thinks to-morrow."

Lastly, reserving the best wine for the conclusion of the feast, there is the proverb that declares the beauty of the women of the County Palatine. "Lancashire fair women" is an article of faith with every Lancashire lad, whether he be of the city or of the bleak fell side. There is no danger of heresy to this complimentary creed, so long as one of the race of Lancashire Witches shall exist.